LAW, CRIME AND LAW ENFORCEMENT

MONEY LAUNDERING

AN ANALYSIS OF FEDERAL LAW

Law, Crime and Law Enforcement

Additional books in this series can be found on Nova's website under the Series tab.

Additional E-books in this series can be found on Nova's website under the E-book tab.

Laws and Legislation

Additional books in this series can be found on Nova's website under the Series tab.

Additional E-books in this series can be found on Nova's website under the E-book tab.

LAW, CRIME AND LAW ENFORCEMENT

MONEY LAUNDERING

AN ANALYSIS OF FEDERAL LAW

CARLYLE M. BENNETT
AND
CARLSON D. TURNER
EDITORS

NOVINKA
New York

For permission to use material from this book please contact us:
Telephone 631-231-7269; Fax 631-231-8175
Web Site: http://www.novapublishers.com

NOTICE TO THE READER

Additional color graphics may be available in the e-book version of this book.

Library of Congress Cataloging-in-Publication Data

ISBN 978-1-62081-614-1

Published by Nova Science Publishers, Inc. †New York

CONTENTS

PREFACE

Money laundering is commonly understood as the process of cleansing the taint from the proceeds of crime. In federal criminal law, however, it is more. In the principal federal criminal money laundering statutes, 18 U.S.C. 1956 and 1957, and to varying degrees in several other federal criminal statutes, money laundering involved the flow of resources to and from several hundred other federal, state, and foreign crimes. Money laundering in some forms is severely punished, sometimes more severely than the underlying crime with which it is associated. The penalties frequently include not only long prison terms, but the confiscation of the property laundered, involved in the laundering, or traceable to the laundering. In this book, an overview of the elements and other legal attributes and consequences of a violation of Sections 1956 and 1957 are discussed, as are select related federal criminal statutes.

Chapter 1 - This is an overview of the elements of federal criminal money laundering statutes and the sanctions imposed for their violation. The most prominent is 18 U.S.C. 1956. Section 1956 outlaws four kinds of money laundering—promotional, concealment, structuring, and tax evasion laundering of the proceeds generated by designated federal, state, and foreign underlying crimes (predicate offenses)—committed or attempted under one or more of three jurisdictional conditions (i.e., laundering involving certain financial transactions, laundering involving international transfers, and stings). Its companion, 18 U.S.C. 1957, prohibits depositing or spending more than $10,000 of the proceeds from a Section 1956 predicate offense. Violations of Section 1956 are punishable by imprisonment for not more than 20 years; Section 1957 carries a maximum penalty of imprisonment for 10 years. Property involved in either case is subject to confiscation. Misconduct which implicates Sections 1956 and 1957 may implicate other federal criminal statutes as well. Federal racketeer influenced and corrupt organization (RICO) provisions outlaw acquiring or conducting the affairs of an enterprise (whose activities affect interstate or foreign commerce) through the patterned commission of a series of underlying federal or state crimes. RICO violations are also 20-year felonies. Every RICO predicate offense, including each "federal crime of terrorism," is automatically a Section 1956 money laundering predicate offense. A second related statute, the Travel Act (18 U.S.C. 1952), punishes interstate or foreign travel, or the use of interstate or foreign facilities, conducted with the intent to distribute the proceeds of a more modest list of predicate offenses or to promote or carry on such offenses when an overt act is committed in furtherance of that intent. Such misconduct is punishable by imprisonment for not more than five years. Other federal statutes proscribe, with varying sanctions, bulk cash smuggling, layering bank deposits to avoid reporting requirements, failure to comply with federal anti-money laundering provisions, or conducting an unlawful money transmission business. The Supreme Court has held that the Section 1956 ban on attempted international transportation of tainted proceeds for the purpose of concealing their ownership, source, nature, or ultimate location is limited to instances where concealment is a purpose rather than an attribute of the transportation (simple smuggling is not proscribed as such), *United States v. Cuellar*, 553 US 550 (2008). In a second case, the Court indicated that for purposes of Section 1956 the "proceeds" of a predicate offense often referred to the profits rather than the gross receipts realized from the offense, *United States v. Santos*, 553 US 507 (2008). Congress responded by defining "proceeds" for purposes of Sections 1956 and 1957 as the property obtained or retained as a consequence of a predicate offense, including gross receipts, P.L. 111-21, 123 Stat. 1618 (2009)(S. 386)(111th Cong.). The text of the statutes discussed, citations of state money laundering and money transmission statutes, a list of Section 1956 federal predicate offenses and their accompanying maximum terms of imprisonment, and a bibliography appear at the end of the report.

Chapter 2 - On June 2, 2008, the U. S. Supreme Court, in *United States v. Santos* (No. 06-1005), vacated convictions of the operator of an illegal lottery and one of his runners who had been charged with conducting financial transactions involving the "proceeds" of an illegal gaming business in violation of 18 U.S.C. § 1956. The ruling is that "proceeds," as used in this money laundering statute, means "profits" rather than "gross receipts" of the underlying unlawful activity. The decision combines a plurality opinion interpreting the word "proceeds" in the statute to mean "profits" and a concurring opinion, necessary for a majority ruling, that leaves room for interpreting "proceeds" as "gross receipts" in other circumstances. A strong dissenting opinion emphasized the constraints the ruling will place on prosecutors. The interpretation rests on two principles of statutory construction: the rule of lenity and the merger doctrine. Under the rule of lenity, ambiguities in criminal statutes are construed in favor of the defendant. Application of the merger doctrine avoids the prospect that a defendant would receive two punishments under different statutes for what is essentially a single offense. On February 5, 2009, Senator Leahy introduced S. 386, the Fraud Enforcement and Recovery Act of 2009, which was reported favorably by the Senate Committee on the Judiciary on March 23, 2009, S.Rept. 111-10. On April 28, the bill, as amended, was passed by the Senate. On May 7, an amended version of the bill was passed by the House. It was returned to the Senate, amended, and passed; thereafter, on May 18, it was passed by the House for presentation to the President. The bill includes provisions amending the definition of "proceeds" under the anti-money laundering criminal statutes, 18 U.S.C. § 1956(c)(8) and 1957(c), to specify that the term includes the "gross receipts" of the underlying criminal activity. As passed by the House, the bill also includes a provision addressing the possibility of a merger problem in money laundering prosecutions for predicate offenses closely connected with the elements of the money laundering offense. Other legislation with provisions to cover "gross receipts" includes S. 378 and H.R. 1793.

In: Money Laundering
Editors: C. Bennett and C. Turner
ISBN 978-1-62081-614-1

Chapter 1

MONEY LAUNDERING: AN OVERVIEW OF 18 U.S.C. 1956 AND RELATED FEDERAL CRIMINAL LAW*

Charles Doyle

SUMMARY

This is an overview of the elements of federal criminal money laundering statutes and the sanctions imposed for their violation. The most prominent is 18 U.S.C. 1956. Section 1956 outlaws four kinds of money laundering—promotional, concealment, structuring, and tax evasion laundering of the proceeds generated by designated federal, state, and foreign underlying crimes (predicate offenses)—committed or attempted under one or more of three jurisdictional conditions (i.e., laundering involving certain financial transactions, laundering involving international transfers, and stings). Its companion, 18 U.S.C. 1957, prohibits depositing or spending more than $10,000 of the proceeds from a Section 1956 predicate offense. Violations of Section 1956 are punishable by imprisonment for not more than 20 years; Section 1957 carries a maximum penalty of imprisonment for 10 years.

Property involved in either case is subject to confiscation. Misconduct which implicates Sections 1956 and 1957 may implicate other federal criminal statutes as well. Federal racketeer influenced and

* This is an edited, reformatted and augmented version of Congressional Research Service, Publication No. RL33315, dated February 8, 2012.

corrupt organization (RICO) provisions outlaw acquiring or conducting the affairs of an enterprise (whose activities affect interstate or foreign commerce) through the patterned commission of a series of underlying federal or state crimes. RICO violations are also 20-year felonies. Every RICO predicate offense, including each "federal crime of terrorism," is automatically a Section 1956 money laundering predicate offense.

A second related statute, the Travel Act (18 U.S.C. 1952), punishes interstate or foreign travel, or the use of interstate or foreign facilities, conducted with the intent to distribute the proceeds of a more modest list of predicate offenses or to promote or carry on such offenses when an overt act is committed in furtherance of that intent. Such misconduct is punishable by imprisonment for not more than five years.

Other federal statutes proscribe, with varying sanctions, bulk cash smuggling, layering bank deposits to avoid reporting requirements, failure to comply with federal anti-money laundering provisions, or conducting an unlawful money transmission business.

The Supreme Court has held that the Section 1956 ban on attempted international transportation of tainted proceeds for the purpose of concealing their ownership, source, nature, or ultimate location is limited to instances where concealment is a purpose rather than an attribute of the transportation (simple smuggling is not proscribed as such), *United States v. Cuellar*, 553 U.S. 550 (2008).

In a second case, the Court indicated that for purposes of Section 1956 the "proceeds" of a predicate offense often referred to the profits rather than the gross receipts realized from the offense, *United States v. Santos*, 553 US. 507 (2008).

Congress responded by defining "proceeds" for purposes of Sections 1956 and 1957 as the property obtained or retained as a consequence of a predicate offense, including gross receipts, P.L. 111-21, 123 Stat. 1618 (2009)(S. 386)(111th Cong.).

The text of the statutes discussed, citations of state money laundering and money transmission statutes, a list of Section 1956 federal predicate offenses and their accompanying maximum terms of imprisonment, and a bibliography appear at the end of the report.

INTRODUCTION

Money laundering is commonly understood as the process of cleansing the taint from the proceeds of crime.[1] In federal criminal law, however, it is more. In the principal federal criminal money laundering statutes, 18 U.S.C. 1956 and 1957, and to varying degrees in several other federal criminal statutes, money laundering involves the flow of resources to and from several hundred other federal, state, and foreign crimes.[2] It consists of:

- engaging in a *financial transaction* involving the proceeds of certain crimes in order *to conceal* the nature, source, or ownership of proceeds they produced;[3]
- engaging in a *financial transaction* involving the proceeds of certain crimes in order *to promote* further offenses;[4]
- *transporting* funds generated by certain criminal activities into, out of, or through the United States in order *to promote* further criminal activities, *or to conceal* the nature, source, or ownership of the criminal proceeds, *or to evade reporting* requirements;[5]
- engaging in a *financial transaction* involving criminal proceeds in order *to evade taxes* on the income produced by the illicit activity;[6]
- *structuring financial transactions* in order to evade reporting requirements;[7]
- *spending more than $10,000* of the proceeds of certain criminal activities;[8]
- *traveling* in, or use of the facilities of, interstate or foreign commerce in order *to distribute* the proceeds of certain criminal activities;[9]
- *traveling* in, or use of the facilities of, interstate or foreign commerce in order to promote certain criminal activities;[10]
- transmitting the proceeds of, or funds to promote, criminal activity in the course of a money transmitting business;[11]
- *transmitting funds* in the course of an unlawful money transmitting business;[12]
- *smuggling* unreported *cash* across a US border;[13] or
- *failing to comply* with the Treasury Department's anti-money laundering provisions.[14]

Money laundering in some forms is severely punished, sometimes more severely than the underlying crime with which it is associated.

The penalties frequently include not only long prison terms, but the confiscation of the property laundered, involved in the laundering, or traceable to the laundering.

This is an overview of the elements and other legal attributes and consequences of a violation of Sections 1956 and 1957, as well as selected related federal criminal statutes.

18 U.S.C. 1956

Section 1956 outlaws four kinds of laundering—promotional, concealment, structuring, and tax evasion—committed or attempted under one or more of three jurisdictional conditions (i.e., laundering involving certain financial transactions, laundering involving international transfers, and stings). More precisely, Section 1956(a)(1)[15] outlaws financial transactions involving the proceeds of other certain crimes—predicate offenses referred to as "specified unlawful activities" (sometimes known as SUA)—committed or attempted (1) with the intent to promote further predicate offenses; (2) with the intent to evade taxation; (3) knowing the transaction is designed to conceal laundering of the proceeds; or (4) knowing the transaction is designed to avoid anti-laundering reporting requirements.

Section 1956(a)(2) outlaws the international transportation or transmission (or attempted transportation or transmission) of funds (1) with the intent to promote a predicate offense; (2) knowing that the purpose is to conceal laundering of the funds and knowing that the funds are the proceeds of a predicate offense; or (3) knowing that the purpose is to avoid reporting requirements and knowing that the funds are the proceeds of a predicate offense. Section 1956(a)(3) is a sting section that covers undercover investigations. It outlaws financial transactions (or attempted transactions) that the defendant believes involve the proceeds of a predicate offense and that are intended to (1) promote a predicate offense, (2) conceal the source or ownership of the proceeds, or (3) avoid reporting requirements.

Promotion

Financial Transactions

Of the three promotional offenses, only the Section 1956(a)(1)(A)(i) financial transaction offense requires use of the proceeds of a predicate offense to promote a predicate offense; the Section 1956 international and sting offenses require only a purpose to promote a predicate offense regardless of the source of the proceeds. Section 1956(a)(1)(A)(i) applies to anyone who:

1. knowing
   A. that the property involved in a financial transaction,
   B. represents the proceeds of some form of unlawful activity,
2. A. conducts or
   B. attempts to conduct such a financial transaction

3 which in fact involves the proceeds of specified unlawful activity
4. with the intent to promote the carrying on of specified unlawful activity.[16]

The knowledge element is the subject of a specific definition which allows a conviction without the necessity of proving that the defendant knew the exact particulars of the underlying offense or even its nature; it is enough that he knew that the property came from some sort of criminal activity and that the property in fact constitutes the proceeds of a predicate offense.[17] The knowledge element cannot be negated by turning a blind eye to reality. Here and throughout Section 1956, knowledge may be inferred from facts indicating that criminal activity is particularly likely.[18]

Throughout Section 1956, a defendant "conducts" a financial transaction when he initiates, concludes, or participates in initiating, or concluding a transaction.[19] The "financial transaction" element has two obvious components. It must be a transaction and it must be financial. Both components are defined by statute. Qualifying "transactions" may take virtually any shape that involves the disposition of something constituting the proceeds of an underlying crime,[20] including disposition as informal as handing cash over to someone else.[21] The "financial" component supplies the jurisdiction foundation for a Section 1956(a)(1)(A)(ii) crime and each of the other crimes in Section 1956(a)(1). Qualifying transactions must either involve the movement of funds in a manner that affects interstate or foreign commerce or involve a financial institution engaged in, or whose activities affect, interstate or foreign commerce.[22] In either case, the effect on interstate or foreign commerce need be no more than de minimis to satisfy the jurisdictional requirement.[23]

The "proceeds" involved in the transaction may consist of "any property derived from or obtained or retained, directly or indirectly, through some form of unlawful activity, including the gross receipts of such activity,"[24] be the property tangible or intangible (*e.g.*, cash or debt), things of value, or things with no intrinsic value (*e.g.*, checks written on depleted accounts).[25]

All but 2 of the 10 Section 1956 crimes are related in one way or another to the commission or purported commission of at least one of a list of predicate offenses, "specified unlawful activities."[26] In the case of the financial institution promotional offense, one of these predicate offenses must be the source of the proceeds used to promote a predicate offense.[27] The predicate offenses come in three varieties: state crimes, foreign crimes, and federal crimes. The list of state crimes is relatively short and consists of any state crime that is a RICO predicate offense,[28] that is, "any act or threat involving murder, kidnapping, gambling, arson, robbery, bribery, extortion, dealing in obscene matter, or dealing in a controlled substance or listed chemical (as defined in section 102 of the Controlled Substances Act), which is chargeable under state law and punishable by imprisonment for more than one year."[29]

The list of foreign crimes recognized as Section 1956 predicate offenses is very much the same— violations of the laws of another country involving murder, kidnapping, bribery, drug trafficking, and the like—but it only applies in cases involving a financial transaction occurring in whole or in part in this country.[30]

The list of federal predicate offenses is considerably longer if for no other reason than it is both specific and generic.[31] For instance, instead of listing "kidnapping in violation of federal law," it lists several of the federal statutes that outlaw kidnapping—interstate kidnapping, kidnapping a Member of Congress, kidnapping the President, and so forth.[32] On the other hand, it also lists "any act or activity constituting an offense involving a federal health care offense."[33] Moreover, it encompasses not only the RICO state predicate offenses but also the RICO federal predicate offenses.[34] The inventory of RICO predicates contains a substantial number of specifically identified federal crimes and any of the federal crimes of terrorism cataloged in 18 U.S.C. 2333b(g)(5)(B).[35]

The courts have struggled with the precise meaning of the interwoven "proceeds" and "promotional " elements of the promotional transaction offense. Under some circumstances, it is difficult to say when the fruits of a crime have been used for further criminal purposes or when the activity is merely part and parcel of the predicate offense. In the Supreme Court's *Santos* case, for instance, the defendant was convicted of running an illegal gambling business in violation of 18 U.S.C. 1955. Section 1955 requires the government to prove that the defendant has conducted a gambling operation either conducted over a 30-day period or one which produced gross revenues of at least $2,000 on any given day. Santos was also convicted of promotional money laundering under Section 1956, based upon evidence that during the course of operations he had paid off his winning customers and paid his employees from the revenue generated by the enterprise.[36] The Court of Appeals decided that these were expenses associated with the commission of the gambling offense, not profits. Proceeds, they reasoned based on their earlier decisions, meant profits, net revenues, not gross revenues (profits and expenses).[37]

Complicating the issue before the Supreme Court was the sentencing disparity between operating a gambling business (a maximum of 5 years imprisonment) and for money laundering (a maximum of 20 years imprisonment). The issue splintered the Court. Four Justices agreed that "proceeds" meant "profits"; four concluded that it meant "gross receipts." The ninth Justice sided with the four "gross receipt" Justices for purposes of the result, but suggested that sometimes proceeds means profits and sometimes it means gross receipts.

Justice Scalia, in the plurality opinion for the Court, noted that the Congress had not at the time explicitly define "proceeds" as the term was used in the money laundering statute.[38] In the absence of a statutory definition, words are thought to have their ordinary meaning. In common parlance, proceeds can mean either profits or gross receipts.[39] When the words of a criminal statute can be read in either of two ways, the rule of lenity requires them to be construed in the manner most favorable to the accused.[40] Recourse to the rule avoids the so-called merger problem:

> Since few lotteries, if any, will not pay their winners, the statute criminalizing illegal lotteries, 18 U.S.C. 1955, would "merge" with the money laundering statute. Congress evidently decided that lottery operators ordinarily deserve up to 5 years of imprisonment, §1955(a), but as a result of merger they would face an additional 20 years [under the money laundering statute], §1956(a)(1).... The merger problem is not limited to lottery operators... Generally speaking, any specified unlawful activity, an episode of which includes transactions which are not elements of the offense and in which the participant passes receipts on to someone else, would merge with money laundering.[41]

Justice Stevens concurred in the result, but not the rationale, of the plurality opinion.[42] He agreed with the dissent at least to the extent that "the legislative history of §1956 makes it clear that Congress intended the term 'proceeds' to include gross revenues from the sale of contraband and the operation of organized crime syndicates involved in such sales."[43] Yet, he found the results of inevitable merger too extraordinary to believe Congress intended them in all instances:

> The revenue generated by a gambling business that is used to pay the essential expenses of operating that business is not "proceeds" within the meaning of the money laundering statute. As the plurality notes, there is "no explanation for why Congress would have wanted a transaction that is a normal part of a crime it had duly considered and appropriately

> punished elsewhere in the Criminal Code, to radically increase the sentence for that crime."... Congress could not have intended the perverse result that would obtain in this case under Justice Alito's opinion.[44]

Consequently, he would presume that Congress intended the word "proceeds" to mean "gross receipts," except in those cases, like *Santos*, where the results would be too "perverse" to support such a presumption.[45]

Speaking for the four dissenters, Justice Alito argued that treating proceeds to mean profits contradicted what Congress probably understood the term to mean.[46] Moreover, since the term applies to both the promotional and concealment offenses, the plurality's result would make it more difficult to prosecute professional money launderers who ordinarily could not be shown to know whether they were laundering gross receipts or only profits.[47] Justice Breyer agreed and added separate dissent contending that the merger problem might better be addressed through the sentencing guidelines or through interpretation of the "promotional" element of the offense.[48]

So what did *Santos* mean? Some courts concluded that its "proceeds means profits" assessment only applied in gambling cases.[49] Others held that it did not apply to cases involving the sale of contraband.[50] Most reasoned that it only applied when there was a risk of merger, a risk that a transaction that was part of the predicate offense would be charged additionally as a money laundering offense.[51]

Congress resolved the issue by adding an explicit definition of proceeds to Section 1956: "the term 'proceeds' means any property derived from or obtained or retained, directly or indirectly, through some form of unlawful activity, *including the gross receipts of such activities*."[52] The definition answers both the profits v. gross receipts question and several others as well. It makes it clear, for example, that the term includes proceeds from a lawful source, retained through the commission of a predicate offense.[53] It does not necessarily invalidate, however, that line of lower court decisions which holds that proceeds must be "derived from an already competed offense, or a completed phase of an ongoing offense, before they can be laundered."[54]

As for the promotional element, some of the lower courts have concluded that it "may be met by transactions that promote the continued prosperity of the underlying offense."[55] One circuit has declared, however, that "the 'promotion' element of money laundering promotion cannot be met simply by demonstrating that the unlawfully earned monies were used to promote the continued functioning of an 'otherwise legitimate business enterprise.' For instance, paying the bills (payroll, rent, taxes) of a health care provider or a car dealership, even one engaged in frequent acts of fraud, may not suffice to support the promotion element."[56]

International Transmission or Transportation

The international promotional offense, Section 1956(a)(2)(A), applies to anyone who:

1. A. transports, transmits, or transfers, or
   B. attempts to transport, transmit, or transfer
2. a monetary instrument or funds
3. A. from a place in the US to or through a place outside the US or
   B. to a place in the US from or through a place outside the US
4. with the intent to promote the carrying on of specified unlawful activity.[57]

"Monetary instruments" is a term defined broadly to include cash, checks, securities, and the like.[58] Since Section 1952(a)(2)(A) proscribes both transportation and attempted transportation, prosecution may be had even though no funds were in fact transported internationally, as long as the government proves a substantial step towards international transportation.[59] The section does not demand that the transported funds flow from a predicate offense or from any other unlawful source; all that is required is that the offender intends to use them to promote a predicate offense.[60] Where the international promotional offense shares common elements with other Section 1956 offenses, they are comparably construed.[61] Thus, similar "intent to promote" elements impose the same requirements of proof upon the government regardless of whether the offense charged is a Section 1956(a)(1)(A)(i) financial transaction promotional offense or a Section 1956(a)(2)(A) international transfer promotional offense.[62] The statutory list of state, federal, and foreign predicate offenses (specified unlawful activities) applies to a Section 1956(a)(2)(A) offense as it does for all but one of the Section 1956 offenses.[63]

Stings

The final promotional money laundering offense, Section 1956(a)(3)(A), is a variation of the financial transaction offense, created to cover situations in which law enforcement officials acting undercover have duped the offender into believing the agent is using the proceeds from a criminal source to promote a predicate offense when in fact he is not.[64] The offense occurs when an offender:

1. with the intent to promote the carrying on of specific unlawful activity
2. A. conducts or
   B. attempts to conduct
3. a financial transaction
4. involving property represented to be
   A. the proceeds of specific unlawful activity or
   B. property used to conduct or facilitate specified unlawful activity.[65]

The generous statutory definition of "financial transactions," which embodies a "sale.... transfer, delivery, or other disposition" involving a monetary instrument or the use of a financial institution, applies with equal force here and throughout Section 1956.[66]

The "representations" alluded to are confined to those "made by a law enforcement officer or by another person at the direction of, or with the approval of, a federal official authorized to investigate or prosecute violations of this section."[67]

In sting prosecutions under other 1956 sections, the courts have held that the representation need not be explicit; it is enough that a reasonable person would infer from the circumstances that funds to be laundered were the proceeds of a predicate offense.[68] The same construction holds true for representations under the financial transaction sting.[69] By definition, the qualifying state, federal, and foreign predicate offenses are the same for Section 1956(a)(3) (A)'s promotional offense stings as for the other Section 1956 offenses.[70]

Prosecution of Section 1956(a)(3) sting offenses might seem to invite entrapment defense claims.

As a general rule, "[w]here the government has induced an individual to break the law and the defense of entrapment is at issue ... the prosecution must prove beyond reasonable doubt that the defendant was predisposed to commit the criminal act prior to first being approached by government agents."[71] Evidence of a defendant's predisposition may include "(1) the character or reputation of the defendant; (2) whether the government made the initial suggestion of criminal activity; (3) whether the defendant engaged in the activity for profit; (4) whether the defendant showed any reluctance; and (5) the nature of the government's inducement."[72] The defense, however, does not appear to have enjoyed a great deal of success in Section 1956(a)(3) cases.[73]

Concealment

Like promotional money laundering, concealment money laundering comes in three varieties; concealment associated with a financial transaction, concealment associated with foreign transportation or transmission, and concealment associated with a sting.

Financial Transactions

Concealment in violation of Section 1956(a)(1)(B)(i) occurs when anyone:

1. knowing
   A. that the property involved in a financial transaction
   B. represents the proceeds of some form of unlawful activity,
2. A. conducts or
   B. attempts to conduct such a financial transaction
3. which in fact involves the proceeds of specified unlawful activity
4. knowing that the transaction is designed in whole or in part to conceal or disguise the nature, location, the source, the ownership, or the control of the proceeds of specified unlawful activity.[74]

The concealment offense shares several common elements with the other offenses in Section 1956. Thus, the defendant must have known that the transaction, designed to conceal, involved crime-tainted proceeds, but need not have known the precise offense or its specifics.[75] Gross receipts of a predicate offense may serve as qualifying "proceeds," for concealment as well as for promotional offenses.[76] The actions that amount to "conduct[ing] or attempt[ing] to conduct" a proscribed transaction—for either concealment or promotional purposes—"include[] initiating, concluding, participating in initiating, or concluding a transaction."[77] The broad definition of "financial transaction" found in Section 1956(c)(4)("sale.... transfer, delivery, or other disposition" involving a monetary instrument or a financial institution) applies throughout the section.[78] As with the promotion offenses, the government must show more than a financial transaction; proof that the defendant spent tainted funds, without more will not do.[79]

In the case of illicit purpose element, the concealment offenses and promotional offenses part company. The promotion offenses speak of the defendant's intent to promote.[80] The concealment offenses speak of the defendant's knowledge of scheme to disguise.[81]

The promotion offenses look to the commission of further predicate offenses; the concealment offenses do not.

The concealment offenses require "a design" to conceal. It is the purpose of scheme and not its effect that the element condemns.[82] A financial transaction that offers neither the accused nor the property involved any apparent enhanced secrecy protection cannot be said to satisfy the intention to conceal element of the offense.[83]

The fact the defendant made no effort to conceal his identity is no defense, however, when the transactions were intended to conceal the nature, location, or origin of the property involved.[84]

As a general matter, "[e]vidence that may be considered when determining whether a transaction was designed to conceal includes: [deceptive] statements by a defendant probative of intent to conceal; unusual secrecy surrounding the transactions; structuring the transaction to avoid attention; depositing illegal profits in the bank account of a legitimate business; highly irregular features of the transaction; using third parties to conceal the real owner; a series of unusual financial moves cumulating in the transaction; and expert testimony on practices of criminals."[85]

Although government need not always prove that a transaction was designed to create the appearance of legitimate wealth, efforts to create such an appearance often signal a money laundering violation.[86]

International Transportation or Transmission

The international concealment offense of Section 1956(a)(2)(B)(i) penalizes anyone who:

1. A. transports, transmits, or transfers, or
   B. attempts to transport, transmit, or transfer
2. a monetary instrument or funds
3. A. from a place in the US to or through a place outside the US or
   B. to a place in the US from or through a place outside the US
4. knowing they came from some form of unlawful activity, and
5. knowing the transportation, transmission, or transfer is designed to conceal or disguise
   A. the nature,
   B. location,
   C. source,
   D. ownership, or
   E. control of
6. the proceeds of a specified unlawful activity.[87]

The standard definitions and construction apply to several of the elements of Section 1956(a)(2)(B)'s international concealment offense. It is the deceptive laundering of the proceeds of state, federal, and foreign predicate offenses that the section proscribes,[88] but only when the proceeds come in the form of "a monetary instrument or funds."[89]

There is no consensus over whether the international money laundering proscriptions of Section 1956(a)(2)(B) reach international transactions that are part of a series of related transactions when the deceptive or evasive transfer in the series is committed entirely either before or after the international transfer.[90]

The Supreme Court, however, has made it clear that the concealment proscribed refers to the purpose for the transportation, not its method.[91] The Court in *Cuellar* held that evidence that the defendant attempted to smuggle cash out of the United States was insufficient to support a prosecution for violation of Section 1956(a)(2)(B)(i), absent evidence of a design to conceal the ownership, source, nature, or ultimate location of the funds.[92]

It made it equally clear, however, that violations are not limited to those instances where the government can establish that the transportation was intended to create the appearance of legitimate wealth.[93]

A drafting quirk casts something of a cloud over the first knowledge element of the Section 1956(a)(2)(B) international transfer offenses ("knowing that the ... *funds* involved in the ... transfer represent the proceeds of some form of unlawful activity").[94]

The statute provides a specific definition for a similar but slightly different phrase used in the financial transaction offenses. The comparable element in the financial transaction offenses of Section 1956(a)(1) refers to *property* in a financial transaction rather than *funds*.[95]

The property phrase ("knowing that the property in a financial transaction") is specifically defined so that the defendant need not know that "unlawful activity" which generates the laundered proceeds constitutes a money laundering predicate offense, that is, a "specified unlawful activity"; it is enough that he knows that it is a state, federal, or foreign felony.[96]

At least one court has held that the same definition applies to Section 1956(a)(2)(B) international offenses notwithstanding the differences in terminology.[97]

Stings

The sting concealment offense in Section 1956(a)(3)(B) is much like the promotional sting offense and occurs when an offender:

1. with the intent to conceal or disguise
    A. the nature,
    B. location,
    C. source,
    D. ownership, or
    E. control of
2. property believed to be the proceeds of a specified unlawful activity
3. A. conducts or
    B. attempts to conduct
3. a financial transaction
4. involving property represented to be
    A. the proceeds of specific unlawful activity or
    B. property used to conduct or facilitate specified unlawful activity.[98]

For purposes of the concealment element of Section 1956(a)(3)(B), exchanging small bills for larger ones may evidence an intent to conceal the location of the proceeds of a predicate offense since a large bill is more easily concealed than the small bills representing an equal amount.[99] Other indicia of an intent to conceal include (1) "unusual secrecy surrounding the transaction," (2) "structuring the transactions to avoid attention," (3) "depositing illegal funds with a legitimate enterprise," (4) "highly irregular features of the transaction," (5) "using third parties to conceal the real owner of the funds," and (6) "unusual financial moves."[100]

The sting proscriptions are found on a belief rather than knowledge that the proceeds involved have been tainted by their involvement in a predicate offense.[101] Nevertheless, a defendant is still not free to turn a blind eye to the fact that the proceeds are represented to have a predicate offense taint.[102]

The "financial transaction" element of the offense demands either a transaction that affects interstate or foreign commerce or a transaction involving the use of a financial institution engaged in or whose activities affect interstate or foreign commerce.[103] To satisfy the "financial institution" prong of the "financial transaction" element of the offense, the government need only establish that the transaction involved "the use of a financial institution" with an interstate or foreign commerce nexus, not that the institution was itself an integral or essential part of the transaction.[104] To satisfy the "transaction" prong, the government need only establish a de minimis effect on interstate commerce.[105]

The representational element does not require undercover agents to have told the defendant in so many words that the transaction involves the proceeds of a predicate offense; it is enough that they "made the defendant aware of circumstances from which a reasonable person would infer that the property was [the proceeds of a predicate offense]."[106]

Evading Reporting Requirements (Smurfing)

Early anti-money laundering efforts sought to enlist the assistance of financial institutions. They were to report large cash transactions to the government.[107] To avoid disclosure of their activities, money launderers sent forth a swarm of subordinates who scurried from bank to bank where they engaged in layered or structured transactions so that no single transaction exceeded the threshold amount of the financial institution's reporting requirements.[108] There are three anti-structuring Section 1956 offenses (sometimes referred to as "smurfing"): one involving financial institutions, one involving international transactions, and one involving stings.[109] The volume of case law, however, suggests that structuring prosecutions are more often brought under 31 U.S.C. 5324, discussed *infra*.

Financial Transactions

The most common of the structuring offenses is that which involves a financial transaction, Section 1956(a)(1)(B)(ii), which forbids:

1. knowing
   A. that the property involved in a financial transaction,
   B. represents the proceeds of some form of unlawful activity,
2. A. conducts or
   B. attempts to conduct such a financial transaction
3. which in fact involves the proceeds of specified unlawful activity
4. with the intent to avoid a state or federal transaction reporting requirement.[110]

Implicit in the intent element is the obligation of the government to establish that the defendant knew of the reporting requirements.[111] The structuring offense described in 31 U.S.C. 5324 requires the government to show that the accused knew that his layering of transactions was unlawful;[112] Section 1956(a)(1)(B)(ii) does not.[113]

The statutory definitions apply equally to the elements of the Section 1956(a)(1)(B)(ii) structuring offense. The phrase "knowing that the property involved in a financial transaction represents the proceeds of some form of unlawful activity" means that the offender must know that the proceeds are derived from some violation of state, federal, or foreign law, but need not know they come from a predicate offense.[114] "Conducts" includes the initiation or participation in a transaction.[115] The required "financial transaction" is any disposition that either affects interstate or foreign commerce or involves either a financial institution engaged in, or whose activities affect, interstate or foreign commerce.[116] The "specified unlawful activities" that must in fact have produced the proceeds involved in the transaction are the same state, federal, and foreign predicate offenses that trigger liability for other offenses in Section 1956.[117]

International Transportation or Transmission

The international smurfing offense of Section 1956(a)(2)(B)(ii) is unusual in that it does not require the presence of proceeds of a predicate offense, as long as the funds are proceeds of some criminal offense. It penalizes anyone who:

1. A. transports, transmits, or transfers, or
   B. attempts to transport, transmit, or transfer
2. a monetary instrument or funds
3. A. from a place in the US to or through a place outside the US or
   B. to a place in the US from or through a place outside the US
4. knowing they represent the proceeds from some form of unlawful activity, and
5. knowing the transportation, transmission, or transfer is designed to avoid a state or federal transaction reporting requirement.[118]

The unlawful activity that generates the proceeds that are the subject of the offense apparently is any felonious violation of state, federal, or foreign law and need not be a predicate offense.[119]

Stings

The sting structuring provision, in contrast, has a predicate offense element:

1. with the intent to avoid a state of federal transaction reporting requirement
2. A. conducts or
   B. attempts to conduct
3. a financial transaction

4. involving property represented to be
A. the proceeds of specific unlawful activity or
B. property used to conduct or facilitate specified unlawful activity.[120]

The representation element may be satisfied by "hints" from undercover officers that the property involved in the transaction comes from a predicate offense; the officers need not have said so in so many words.[121]

Tax Evasion

The tax evasion money laundering offense must be tethered to a financial transaction, 18 U.S.C. 1956(a)(1)(A)(ii); there is no international or undercover counterpart.

Financial Transactions

Money laundering for tax evasion purposes occurs whenever a person:

1. knowing
   A. that the property involved in a financial transaction,
   B. represents the proceeds of some form of unlawful activity,
2. A. conducts or
   B. attempts to conduct such a financial transaction
3. which in fact involves the proceeds of specified unlawful activity
4. with the intent to engage in conduct in violation of 26 U.S.C. 7201 (attempt to evade or defeat tax) or 7206 (tax fraud or false tax statements).[122]

A tax evasion, laundering prosecution requires the government to show that the defendant acted intentionally rather than inadvertently, but not that the defendant knew that his conduct violated the tax laws.[123]

Conspiracy, Attempt, Aiding and Abetting

Each of the 10 criminal proscriptions found in Section 1956 outlaws both the completed offense and the attempt to commit it.[124] Attempt adds an additional feature to the underlying offense, the government must establish that the defendant's action constituted a "substantial step" towards the commission of a completed offense.[125]

Conspiracy to commit a federal crime is a separate federal offense punishable by imprisonment for not more than five years.[126] In addition, Section 1956(h) declares that "[a]ny person who conspires to commit any offense defined in this section or section 1957 shall be subject to the same penalties as those prescribed for the offense the commission of which was the object of the conspiracy."[127] Although a casual reading might indicate that Section 1956(h) simply changes the penalty for a Section 371 conspiracy to violate Section 1956 to match the other penalties for violation Section 1956, Section 1956(h) in fact creates a separate crime.[128] The distinction matters because violation of Section 371 is not complete until one of the conspirators commits an overt act in furtherance of the scheme;[129] Section 1956(h) has no such overt act requirement.[130] Conspiracy to violate Section 1956 carries with it the prospect of liability for any foreseeable offenses committed by co-conspirators in furtherance of the scheme.[131]

The confluence of the language of Section 1956(h) and that of the substantive offenses in Section 1956, each of which contains an attempt component, raises the curious possibility of a prosecution of conspiracy to attempt a violation of one of the substantive offenses. Although the case law is sparse, the courts appear to have acknowledged that "conspiracy to attempt" may constitute an indictable offense both as a general matter and in the case of Section 1956.[132] The cases, however, do not discuss the offense's precise elements. Attempt ordinarily requires proof of a substantial step towards the completion of the underlying offense; conspiracy to attempt, whether in the absence of an overt act requirement or not, presumably requires something less.

As a general matter, anyone who commands, counsels, or aids and abets the commission of a federal crime by another is equally culpable and equally punishable.[133] "In order to aid and abet another to commit a crime it is necessary that a defendant in some sort associated himself with the venture, that he participated in it as in something that he wishes to bring about, that he seek by his action to make it succeed."[134]

Consequences

Prison terms, fines, restitution, confiscation, and civil penalties may follow as a consequence of conviction of a money laundering offense.

Imprisonment

Any violation of Section 1956 is punishable by imprisonment for not more than 20 years.[135] The first sentencing guidelines reflected the fact that Section 1956 was a 20-year felony and the anticipation that the section would apply primarily in cases in which drug trafficking and organized crime offenses were the predicate offenses.[136] Thereafter, the Sentencing Commission became concerned about the application of the initial guidelines in cases involving less severely punished predicate offenses such as mail fraud.[137] Subsequent amendments to the guidelines[138] and penalty increases in some of the predicate offenses[139] address that concern. Defendants sentenced to a term of imprisonment may also be subject a term of supervised released of up to three years to be served upon their release from prison.[140]

Fines and Civil Penalties

Violations of Section 1956(a)(1) and (a)(2), the financial institution and interstate or foreign transmission offenses, are punishable by a fine of no more than the greater of $500,000 or twice the value of the property involved in the offense.[141] Sting violations are punishable by a fine of not more than the greater of $250,000 ($500,000 for an organization) or twice the amount involved in the offense.[142] Violators of any provisions of Section 1956 are subject to a civil penalty of no more than the greater of $10,000 or the value of the property involved in the offense.[143]

Forfeiture

Forfeiture is the confiscation of property to the government as a consequence of the property's proximity to some form of criminal activity.[144] The government's claim to the property can be secured by default or through judicial proceedings conducted either civilly and ordinarily *in rem* (against the property itself) or as part of the criminal proceedings against the property owner.[145]

The proceeds of a confiscation are generally shared among the law enforcement agencies that participate in the investigation and prosecution of the forfeiture.[146]

Section 1956 provides a vehicle for civil or criminal confiscation in two very distinct ways. First, the "proceeds" of any Section 1956 predicate offense (and any property traceable to such proceeds) are subject to confiscation without the necessity of any actual violation of Section 1956.[147]

This permits the confiscation of property derived from crimes that might form the basis for a money laundering offense without having to prove that a money laundering offense occurred.[148] Second, property "involved" in a Section 1956 money laundering offense (or property traceable to such involved property) may be confiscated.[149]

Involved property obviously includes more than the proceeds of the predicate offense, since the proceeds are separately forfeitable already. "Property eligible for forfeiture under 18 U.S.C. §982(a)(1) includes that money or property which was actually laundered ... , along with any commissions or fees paid to the launderer and any property used to facilitate the laundering offense."[150]

In theory, confiscation might dip into both sides of a tainted transaction, the proceeds from the predicate offense and the cashier's check, real estate, jewelry, or sports car purchased with the proceeds in a laundering transaction. In practice, however, involved property has been construed to mean untainted property joined with the proceeds of a predicate offense as part of the laundering transaction.[151]

Property acquired in exchange for the proceeds or for the proceeds and other involved property is forfeitable as traceable property. The government may confiscate the property on either side of the transaction, but not the property on both sides.[152]

The Eighth Amendment prohibits excessive fines. Fines are excessive if they are grossly disproportionate to the gravity of the offender's misconduct.[153]

While the excessive fines clause may impose limits upon the permissible extent of the confiscation for failure to comply with anti-money laundering reporting statutes,[154] forfeitures under Section 1956 are not ordinarily considered excessive because of the gravity of the offense and its predicate offenses.[155]

Venue

The Constitution guarantees the accused the right to trial in the state in which the crime charged was committed and before a jury from the state and district in which the crime was committed.[156]

In *United States v. Cabrales*,[157] the defendant was tried in Missouri for laundering, in Florida, the proceeds of a Missouri drug dealing ring.

The Supreme Court held the Constitution precludes trial of a money laundering charge in the district in which the predicate offense occurred unless the laundering and the predicate offense occurred in the same district or perhaps unless the launderer was a co-conspirator in the commission of the predicate offense or participated in the transfer of the laundered property from the place where the predicate offense occurred (*e.g.*, Missouri) to the place where the laundering occurred (*e.g.*, Florida).[158]

The Section 1956 money laundering venue provision was amended with an eye to the Court's decision.[159]

18 U.S.C. 1957

Elements

Unless there is some element of promotion, concealment, or evasion, Section 1956 does not make a separate crime of simply spending or depositing tainted money. Section 1957 does.[160] It outlaws otherwise innocent transactions contaminated by the origin of the property involved in the transaction.[161] Using most of the same definitions as Section 1956, the elements of 1957 cover anyone who:

1. A. in the United States,
   B. in the special maritime or territorial jurisdiction of the United States, or
   C. outside the United States if the defendant is an American,
2. knowingly
3. A. engages or
   B. attempts to engage in
4. a monetary transaction
5. [in or affecting US interstate or foreign commerce]
6. in criminally derived property that
   A. is of a greater value than $10,000 and
   B. is derived from specified unlawful activity.[162]

The courts often supply an abbreviated statement of the crime's elements. To prove money laundering under §1957, the government must prove: "(1) that the defendant engaged in or attempted to engage in a monetary transaction, (2) in criminally derived property worth at least $10,000; (3) with knowledge that the property was derived from unlawful activity, and (4) the property is, in fact, derived from specified unlawful activity."[163]

At the heart of any Section 1957 offense lies a monetary transaction. A monetary transaction for purposes of Section 1957 is a financial transaction as understood under Section 1956[164] or any other deposit or transfer of cash or check or the like, in or affecting interstate or foreign commerce and involving a financial institution.[165] Section 1957 only applies to transactions involving $10,000 or more *at the time of the transaction.*[166] Numbered among the qualifying financial institutions are banks and credit unions, but also car dealerships, jewelers, casinos, stockbrokers, travel agents, and pawnbrokers, to mention a few.[167] The government's jurisdictional burden is comparable to the one it must bear for Section 1956 (a transaction in or affecting interstate or foreign commerce or one involving a financial institution) and demands evidence of only a slight impact on commerce.[168]

The government must prove that the defendant knew the property in the transaction was the product of some criminal activity,[169] but it need not show that he knew that it was the product of a "specified unlawful activity."[170] Section 1957(f)(2) describes "criminally derived property" as "any property derived from or obtained or retained, directly or indirectly, through some form of unlawful activity, including the gross receipts of such activity." Of course, the property must in fact be derived from a specified unlawful activity (predicate offense),[171] and Section 1957 uses the definition of specified unlawful activities from Section 1956.[172]

Section 1957 contains an attorney's fee exception. It excludes from the "monetary transaction" element of the offense "any transaction necessary to preserve a person's right to representation as guaranteed by the sixth amendment to the Constitution."[173] The exception, however, reach no more than an individual's payment of services covered by the Sixth Amendment.[174] It creates a safe harbor against prosecutions under Section 1957, but is no defense to a charge of promotional, concealment, or evasive money laundering under Section 1956.[175]

Attempt, Conspiracy, Aiding and Abetting

Section 1957 proscribes attempts to violate its provisions.[176] As a general rule, attempt requires proof of an intent to commit the underlying offense and the commission of a substantial step towards its completion.[177]

The general rules apply with respect to attempts to commit the offenses under Section 1956,[178] and there is every reason to believe they apply to attempts to commit a violation of Section 1957.

Section 1956(h) outlaws conspiracy to violate Section 1957. A conviction for conspiracy to violate the section requires the government to prove: "(1) there was an agreement between two or more persons to commit money laundering and (2) that the defendant joined the agreement knowing its purpose and with the intent to further the illegal purpose."[179] Section 1956(h) creates a crime which requires no proof of an overt act in furtherance of the conspiracy.[180]

In addition to the conspiracy offense, conspirators are liable for the foreseeable offenses committed by coconspirators in furtherance of the scheme.[181] Those who aid or abet the money laundering of another are likewise liable as though they had committed the offense themselves.[182]

Consequences

Imprisonment

Violation of Section 1957 and conspiracy to violate Section 1957 are each punishable by imprisonment for not more than 10 years. Under the sentencing guidelines, many offenders will be ineligible for a sentence of probation even as part of a split sentence.[183] Where probation is available and imposed, the term must be not less than one nor more than five years.[184] If imprisoned, offenders may also be subject to a term of supervised release of up to three years to be served upon their release from prison.[185]

Fines

Violation of Section 1957 and conspiracy to violate Section 1957 are each punishable by a fine of not more than the greater of $250,000 ($500,000 for an organization) or twice the amount involved in the transaction.[186] Violators of Section 1957 are subject to a civil penalty of no more than the greater of $10,000 or the value of the property involved in the offense.[187]

Forfeiture

Any property involved in a violation of Section 1957 or traceable to property involved in a violation of Section 1957 is subject to confiscation under either civil or criminal procedures, and the applicable law is essentially the same as in the case of Section 1956.[188]

18 U.S.C. 1952: Travel Act

The Travel Act, 18 U.S.C. 1952, is one of the older members of the family of money laundering related criminal statutes. While Sections 1956 and 1957 punish transactions involving promoting, concealing, spending, and depositing tainted funds, the Travel Act punishes interstate or foreign travel (or use of the facilities of interstate or foreign commerce) conducted with the intent to (1) distribute the proceeds of a more modest list of predicate offenses ("unlawful activity"), or (2) to promote or carry on such offenses when there is overt act in furtherance of that intent, or (3) to commit some violent act in their furtherance. The first two variants bear some resemblance to the concealment and promotion offenses of Section 1956 and somewhat more remotely to the deposit/spending proscriptions of Section 1957. The violent crime component of the Travel Act is only coincidentally related to money laundering and consequently will be mentioned only in passing.

The Travel Act's elements cover anyone who:

1. A. travels in interstate or foreign commerce, or
   B. uses any facility in interstate or foreign commerce, or
   C. uses the mail
2. with intent
   A. to distribute the proceeds of an unlawful activity, i.e.,
      i. any business enterprise involving unlawful activities gambling, moonshining, drug dealing, or prostitution; or
      ii. extortion, bribery, or arson; or
      iii. any act which is indictable as money laundering; or
   B. commit an act of violence to further an unlawful activity; or
   C. to otherwise
      i. promote,
      ii. manage,
      iii. establish,
      iv. carry on, or
      v. facilitate the promotion, management, establishment, or carrying on any unlawful activity; and
3. thereafter
   A. distributes or attempts to distribute such proceeds, or
   B. commits or attempts to commit such act of violence, or
   C. promotes, manages, establishes, carries on, or facilitates the promotion, management, establishment, or carrying on such unlawful activities or attempts to do so.[189]

Distribution, Facilitation, and Violence

The courts often abbreviate their statement of the elements to encompass only whichever of the three versions is at issue:

> *Distribution*—The essential elements of a violation under section 1952(a) are: "(1) travel in interstate or foreign commerce; (2) with the specific intent to distribute the proceeds of an unlawful activity; and (3) knowing and willful commission of an act in furtherance of that intent."[190]
>
> *Facilitation*—The government must prove that the defendant "(1) travels in interstate or foreign commerce [or uses an interstate facility] (2) with intent to ... promote ... any unlawful activity and (3) that the

defendant thereafter performs or attempts to perform an act of promotion ... of any unlawful activity."[191]

Violence—"To prove a violation of the Travel Act, the government was required to establish that Ajaj: (1) used a facility of interstate or foreign commerce; (2) with intent to commit any unlawful activity (including arson...); and (3) thereafter performed an additional act to further the unlawful activity.[192]

The accused need not have been guilty of the unlawful activities that generated the distributed proceeds.[193] "Distribution" in Section 1952(a)(1) "carries a connotation of distribution of illegal proceeds to persons in organized crime conspiracies. Certainly the person receiving them must be entitled to them for reasons other than normal and otherwise lawful purchase and sale of goods at market prices."[194] Distribution, however, does include distribution to "pay off" criminal associates,[195] as well as the interstate transfer of criminal proceeds to a confederate for the purchase of controlling interest in a bank in order to facilitate subsequent laundering.[196] Actual distribution is not necessary for conviction; the offense simply involves interstate commerce; an intent to distribute; and a subsequent attempt to distribute, some action—perhaps incomplete or unsuccessful—in furtherance of the intent to distribute.[197]

The dimensions of the facilitation offense are comparable. In addition to interstate travel or the use of interstate facilities with the requisite intent, it requires the performance or attempted performance of some subsequent overt act in furtherance of the intent to "promote, manage, establish, carry on, or facilitate the promotion, management, establishment or carrying on" of a predicate offense such as a business enterprise involving drug dealing.[198]

Since the statute condemns attempt and promotion rather than commission of a predicate act, the overt act need not constitute a completed predicate offense.[199]

Travel

Common to each of the three offenses is the jurisdictional element: interstate or foreign travel or the use of the mail or some other facility of interstate or foreign travel. When the Travel Act's jurisdictional element involves mail or facilities in interstate or foreign commerce, rather than interstate travel, evidence that a telephone was used,[200] or an ATM,[201] or the facilitates of an interstate banking chain[202] will do.[203] The government is not required to show that the defendant used the facilities himself or that the use was critical to the success of the criminal venture. It is enough that he caused them to be used[204] and that their employment was useful for his purposes.[205]

Unlawful Activity

Predicate offenses (unlawful activity) are likewise common to the Travel Act's proceeds distribution, violence in furtherance, and promotional offenses. The Travel Act's predicate offenses come in three stripes—money laundering offenses; extortion-bribery-arson offenses; and offenses of the gambling, prostitution, drug dealing, and bootlegging "businesses." The money laundering predicate offenses include Sections 1956 and 1957 as well as the currency transaction reporting offenses.[206]

The second class of Travel Act predicate offenses consists simply of the crimes of extortion, bribery, or arson committed in violation of state or federal law, 18 U.S.C. 1952(b)(2). The terms "extortion," "bribery," and "arson" as they appear in the Travel Act are generic; they mean what they were commonly understood to mean when the Travel Act was enacted, even if the common law definition is more restrictive or if the state law which proscribes them uses a different name.[207]

The final class of Travel Act predicates is more restrictive. It encompasses gambling, prostitution, drug dealing, and certain forms of tax evasion only when committed in conjunction with a "business enterprise."[208] A criminal business enterprise, as understood in the Travel Act, "contemplates a continuous course of business—one that already exists at the time of the overt act or is intended thereafter. Evidence of an isolated criminal act, or even sporadic acts, will not suffice,"[209] and it must be shown to be involved in an unlawful activity outlawed by a specifically identified state or federal statute.[210]

Conspiracy, Aiding and Abetting

Attempt is not a separate Travel Act offense, but accomplice and co-conspirator liability, discussed earlier, apply with equal force to the Travel Act.[211]

Consequences

The distribution and facilitation offenses of the Travel Act, 18 U.S.C. 1952(a)(1) and 18 U.S.C. 1952(a)(3), are punishable by imprisonment for not more than five years.[212] The crime of violence offense is punishable by imprisonment for not more than 20 years, or by imprisonment for life or any term of years if death results.[213] Offenders of any of the three offenses are subject to a fine of the greater of not more than $250,000 ($500,000 for organizations) or twice the gain or loss associated with the offense.[214] If imprisoned, offenders may also be subject to a term of supervised release of up to three years to be served upon their release from prison.[215] Property associated with a violation of Section 1952 is not subject to confiscation solely by virtue of that fact,[216] although the property may be confiscated by operation of the laws governing Section 1952 predicate offense or by operation of RICO or the money laundering provisions. For example, interstate travel conducted with the intent to distribute drug trafficking proceeds involving an act in furtherance of that intent is a violation of Section 1952. The proceeds are not subject to forfeiture as a consequence, but they are subject to confiscation by operation of the forfeiture provisions of the Controlled Substances Act.[217] Moreover, Travel Act violations have been designated RICO predicate offenses and consequently qualify as money laundering predicates under Sections 1956 and 1957.[218] Thus, to the extent that Travel Act proceeds are involved in a financial transaction or monetary transaction in violation of Section 1956 or 1957, they are subject to confiscation.[219]

31 U.S.C. 5322: Reporting Requirements

Section 5322 penalizes willful violation of several monetary transaction reporting requirements found primarily in Subtitle 53-II of title 31 of the United States Code.[220] The section's coverage extends to violations of:

-31 U.S.C. 5313—financial institution reports of cash transactions involving $10,000 or more (31 C.F.R. §103.22);

-31 U.S.C. 5314—reports by persons in the US of foreign financial agency transactions (31 C.F.R. §103.24);

-31 U.S.C. 5316—reports by any person taking $10,000 in cash out of the US or bring it in;

-31 U.S.C. 5318—suspicious transaction reports by financial institutions;

-31 U.S.C. 5318A—special measures record keeping and reports by financial institutions relating to foreign counter-money laundering concerns;

-31 U.S.C. 5325—reports by financial institutions issuing cashier's checks in amounts of $3000 or more (31 C.F.R. §103.29);

-31 U.S.C. 5326—cash transaction reports by financial institutions and/or various trades or businesses pursuant to Treasury Department geographical orders (31 C.F.R. §103.26);

-31 U.S.C. 5331—reports of trades and businesses other than financial institutions of cash transactions involving $10,000 or more (31 C.F.R. §103.30);

-12 U.S.C. 1829b—record keeping requirements of federally insured depository institutions;

-12 U.S.C. 1953—record keeping by uninsured banks or similar institutions.

Section 5322 does not cover violations of Section 5315 (relating to foreign currency transaction reports) which are subject to the civil penalty provisions of 31 U.S.C. 5321 or of Section 5324 (relating to structuring financial transactions) which carries its own criminal penalties.

Simple violations of Section 5322 are punishable by imprisonment for not more than five years, a fine of not more than $250,000, or both.[221] Violations committed during the commission of another federal crime or as part of a pattern of illegal activity involving more than $100,000 over the course of a year are punishable by imprisonment for not more than 10 years; a fine of not more than $500,000 (not more than $1 million for a special measures violation (31 U.S.C. 5318A) or a violation involving a breach of due diligence with respect to private banking for foreign customers or foreign shell banks (31 U.S.C. 5318(i), (j)); or both.[222]

In order to establish "willful" violation of Section 5322, the government must prove that the accused knew that his breach of the statute was unlawful.[223]

Section 5322 is a Travel Act predicate offense. It is also RICO predicate offense,[224] consequently a Section 1956 or 1957 money laundering predicate offense.[225] Property associated with violations of two of the sections within its coverage is subject to confiscation.[226] Under Section 5317(c), property becomes forfeitable when it is involved in, or traceable to, a violation of 31 U.S.C. 5313 (reports relating to cash transactions involving $10,000 or more) or of 31 U.S.C. 5316 (reports relating to taking $10,000 or more out of the US or to bring it into the US). The confiscation, however, may be subject to a constitutional excessive fine limitation.[227] In *United States v. Bajakajian*,[228] the Supreme Court held that the confiscation of $357,144 for a violation of 31 U.S.C. 5322 occasioned by a failure to comply with the reporting requirements of 31 U.S.C. 5316 would constitute an unconstitutionally excessive fine—in the absence of evidence that the money was derived from, or destined to facilitate, some other criminal activity. In later cases involving the failure to report transported cash, the courts have occasionally ordered confiscation of less than all of the unreported cash if the total was substantial and the cash was otherwise untainted.[229] In most instances, however, *Bajakajian* appears to pose little obstacle to complete or near complete forfeiture.[230]

31 U.S.C. 5324: Anti-Structuring

When Congress established the general anti-structuring provisions of Section 1956 in 1986,[231] it also created a more specific anti-structuring offense, 31 U.S.C. 5324.[232] Prior to that time, it was a crime for a financial institution to fail to report a cash transaction involving more than $10,000.[233] Yet there was no explicit prohibition against an individual breaking a transaction into several smaller transactions in order to avoid triggering the bank's reporting requirement, although such structuring could sometimes be prosecuted as a conspiracy to defraud the federal government.[234]

From the beginning, Section 5324 condemned causing the failure to file a required report, causing the submission of a false report, structuring transactions to evade a reporting requirement, or attempting to do so.[235] Its growth over the years has been the product primarily of protecting a wider range of reporting systems than was originally the case. Its proscriptions are now divided into three sections according to the type of reporting or record keeping involved: one is devoted to transactions involving banks, credit unions, car dealerships, jewelers, casinos, and the other similar entities classified as financial institutions;[236] another to cash transactions of $10,000 or more involving nonfinancial institutions;[237] and a third to bringing $10,000 or more in cash into the country or taking it out of the country.[238] But the prohibitions remain the same. No person may cause the failure to submit a required report, or cause the submission of a false report, or structure their transactions to evade a reporting requirement, or attempt to do so.[239] The prohibitions extend to instances of breaking a single transaction in several smaller transactions, but also reach instances of breaking a cash transaction into a mix of cash, check, and/or credit payments.[240]

Violations are punishable by imprisonment for not more than five years (not more than 10 years if committed in conjunction with another federal offense or if committed as part of a pattern of activity involving $100,000 or more) and a fine of not more than $250,000 (not more than $500,000 for organizations), with the fine maximum doubled if the offense is committed in conjunction with another federal crime or as part of a pattern of activity involving $100,000.[241]

Any property involved in a structuring violation of the section is subject to confiscation.[242] Such forfeitures do not offend the Eighth Amendment's excessive fines clause unless they are grossly disproportionate to the gravity of the offense.[243]

For some time, Section 5324 simply housed prohibitions and Congress relied upon Section 5322 to provide the criminal sanctions for violations of the Section 5324 prohibitions, as well as for the other prohibitions in subchapter 53 II of title 31 of the US Code. Then as now, Section 5322 condemned only willful violations.[244] Congress removed Section 5324 from the coverage of Section 5322 and provided criminal penalties within Section 5324 in 1994[245] after the Supreme Court held that "willful" violation required a showing that the defendant knew that his structuring actions were unlawful.[246] Thus for a prosecution under Section 5324, it is no longer necessary to prove that the accused knew that his conduct was criminal; it is enough to show that he knew of the reporting requirement and acted with an intent to avoid compliance or accurate compliance.[247]

31 U.S.C. 5332: Bulk Cash Smuggling

After the Supreme Court held in *Bajakajian* that the excessive fines clause of the Eighth Amendment precluded confiscation of $300,000 of unreported, but otherwise untainted, cash,[248]

Congress enacted the bulk cash smuggling provisions of 31 U.S.C. 5332. The section outlaws carrying or attempting to transport more than $10,000 in unreported, "concealed" cash across a US border with the intent to evade 31 U.S.C. 5316 reporting requirements.[249]

The section has been used to prosecute those who attempted to bring unreported cash into the United States, as well as those who attempted to smuggle cash out of the country.[250] The fact that the money was neither derived from criminal activity nor intended for criminal purposes may be relevant for Eighth Amendment purposes, but it is no defense to the underlying offense.[251]

The proscribed methods of concealment seem to envelope any method short of public display.[252] The offense carries a prison term of not more than five years, but also calls for confiscation of the cash and related property in lieu of a fine.[253] The section was apparently enacted to overcome the consequences of *Bajakajian*.[254] There may be some question whether the effort will succeed.[255]

18 U.S.C. 1960: Money Transmitters

Section 1960 outlaws conducting or owning an unlicensed money transmitting business.[256] "Money transmitting" is defined broadly by way of a nonexclusive list of examples, such as checks and wire transfers.[257] The term the term "business" restricts the offense to an enterprise conducted for profit and one engaged in more than a single qualifying transmission.[258]

The section recognizes three categories of transmitting business.[259] One consists of any transmission business operating in a state that requires it to be licensed and criminalizes the failure to do so.[260] Here, the government must prove that the defendant knew that he was conducting a money transmitting business and that it was unlicensed.[261] It need not prove the defendant knew that state require him to seek a license or of the state criminal penalty for transmission without a license.[262]

The second category of unlicensed money transmitting businesses consists of any transmitting business operating in a manner that fails to comply with Treasury Department regulations governing such enterprises.[263] Here, the government need not show that the defendant knew of federal regulatory requirements,[264] but it must show that the defendant knew that he was operating a transmitting business.[265] The third category consists of any licensed business that transmits of money known to be derived from or intended to finance criminal activity even if the transmitter is duly licensed.[266]

Section 1960 offenses are punishable by imprisonment for not more than five years and/or a fine of not more than $250,000 (not more than $500,000 for organizations).[267] Property "involved in" violation of the section is subject to civil and criminal forfeiture.[268] The section has withstood challenges arguing that it is unconstitutionally vague.[269]

Racketeer Influenced and Corrupt Organizations (RICO)

As noted earlier, all RICO predicate offenses are by definition money laundering predicate offenses under Sections 1956 and 1957.[270] The crimes that suggest the possibility of a RICO offense also suggest the possibility of money laundering. In some money laundering cases, although there is no separate RICO violation, prosecution is possible by virtue of the RICO shared predicate offense list.[271] In a number of other cases, either money laundering is one of several predicate offenses of a larger RICO enterprise[272] or the RICO enterprise is devoted primarily to money laundering.[273]

RICO makes it a federal crime for any person to:

1. conduct or participate, directly or indirectly, in the conduct of
2. the affairs of an enterprise
3. engaged in or the activities of which affect, interstate or foreign commerce
4. A. through the collection of an unlawful debt, or
   B. through a pattern of racketeering activity (predicate offenses).[274]

In other words, "[f]or a defendant to convicted of a substantive RICO offense [under section 1962(c)], the government must prove the following elements beyond a reasonable doubt: (1) the existence of an enterprise; (2) that affected interstate commerce; and (3) that the defendant associated with the enterprise; (4) and conducted or participated in the conduct of the enterprise; (5) through a pattern of racketeering activity."[275]

This statement of the elements addresses the more common RICO prosecution involving a pattern of racketeering activity (i.e., predicate offenses), but the government is under no obligation to prove pattern if the underlying misconduct is "the collection of an unlawful debt."[276]

The "person" who commits a RICO offense need not be a human being, but may be "any individual or entity capable of holding a legal or beneficial interest in property."[277]

The "enterprise" element is defined with comparable breadth, embracing "any individual, partnership, corporation, association, or other legal entity, and any union or group of individuals associated in fact although not a legal entity."[278] In spite of their sweeping scope, the elements are distinct, and a single defendant may not be simultaneously charged as both the "person" and the "enterprise" under 18 U.S.C. 1962(c).[279]

Subject to this limitation, however, a RICO enterprise may be formal or informal, legal or illegal. In order for a group associated in fact to constitute a RICO enterprise, the group need not have obvious hierarchical or business-like structure; it need only be characterized by "at least three structural features: a purpose, relationships among those associated with the enterprise, and longevity sufficient to permit those associates to pursue the enterprise's purpose."[280]

The interstate commerce element of the RICO offense may be established by evidence that the enterprise either has conducted its affairs in interstate commerce or foreign commerce or has engaged in activities that affect interstate commerce or foreign commerce.[281]

The "pattern of racketeering activity" element demands the commission of at least two predicate offenses,[282] which must be of sufficient relationship and continuity to be described as a "pattern."[283]

Related crimes, for pattern purposes, are marked by "the same or similar purposes, results, participants, victims, or methods of commission, or otherwise are interrelated by distinguishing characteristics and are not isolated events."[284]

The "continuity" of predicate offenses may be shown in two ways, either by proof of the regular occurrence of related misconduct over an extended period of time in the past (closed ended) or by evidence of circumstances suggesting that if not stopped by authorities, they would have continued in the future (open ended).[285]

The courts have been reluctant to find the continuity required for a RICO pattern for past, closed ended enterprises (those with no threat of future predicate offenses) unless the enterprise's activities spanned a fairly long period of time.[286]

Open ended continuity (found where there is a threat of future predicate offenses) is nowhere near as time sensitive and is often found where the predicates consist of murder, drug dealing or the like, or are part of the enterprise's regular way of doing business.[287]

Section 1962(d) also outlaws conspiracy to violate any of Section 1962's substantive prohibitions; in the case of conspiracy to violate Section 1962(c), it outlaws any agreement of two or more to conduct the affairs of an enterprise through a pattern of RICO predicate offenses.[288]

The RICO conspiracy offense has no overt act requirement; the crime is complete upon the agreement to commit a RICO offense.[289]

RICO violations are punishable by imprisonment for not more than 20 years (not more than life imprisonment if any of the applicable predicate offenses carries a life sentence).[290]

Offenders also face fines of up to $250,000 (up to $500,000 for organizations) as well as the confiscation of any property associated with the offense.[291]

They may also be liable to their victims for triple damages and reasonable attorneys fees.[292]

Depending upon the circuit, they may also be subject to equitable remedies,[293] and may be liable even if they only aided and abetted the underlying RICO violation.[294]

SPECIFIED UNLAWFUL ACTIVITIES (CITATIONS TO PREDICATE OFFENSES: 18 U.S.C. 1956, 1957) (MAXIMUM TERMS OF IMPRISONMENT NOTED)

-7 U.S.C. 2024 (Food Stamp Act of 1977 felony (violation involving a quantity of coupons having a value of not less than $5,000)) (various from 1 to 20 years);

-8 U.S.C. 1324 (bringing in and harboring certain aliens (committed for the purpose of financial gain)) (various from 5 years to life);*[295]

-8 U.S.C. 1327 (aiding or assisting certain aliens to enter the United States (committed for the purpose of financial gain)) (10 years);*

-8 U.S.C. 1328 (importation of alien for immoral purpose (committed for the purpose of financial gain)) (10 years);*

-15 U.S.C. 77a et seq. (fraud in the sale of securities) (5 years);*

-15 U.S.C. 78ff (Foreign Corrupt Practices Act felony) (various from 5 to 20 years);

-18 U.S.C. 32 (destruction of aircraft) (20 years);[296]

-18 U.S.C. 37 (violence at international airports) (20 years);

-18 U.S.C. 81 (arson within special maritime and territorial jurisdiction) (25 years);**[297]

-18 U.S.C. 115 (influencing, impeding, or retaliating against a Federal official by threatening or injuring a family member) (various from 1 to 30 years);

-18 U.S.C. 152 (concealment of assets; false oaths and claims; bribery) (5 years);

-18 U.S.C. 175-178 (biological weapons) (various from 5 years to life);*

-18 U.S.C. 175c (variola virus) (various from 25 years to life);

-18 U.S.C. 201 (bribery) (various from 2 to 15 years);*

-18 U.S.C. 215 (commissions or gifts for procuring loans) (various 1 to 30 years);

-18 U.S.C. 224 (sports bribery) (5 years);*

-18 U.S.C. 229-229F (chemical weapons) (life);*

-18 U.S.C. 287 (federal health care offense relating to a benefit program) (5 years);

-18 U.S.C. 351 (violence against Members of Congress or Cabinet officers) (various from 1 year to life);

-18 U.S.C. 371 (conspiracy to commit a federal health care offense) (5 years);~[298]

-18 U.S.C. 471, 472, and 473 (counterfeiting) (20 years);*
-18 U.S.C. 500-503 (certain counterfeiting offenses) (5 years);
-18 U.S.C. 541 (goods falsely classified) (2 years);
-18 U.S.C. 542 (entry of goods by means of false statements) (2 years);
-18 U.S.C. 544 (smuggling goods from the United States) (2 years);
-18 U.S.C. 545 (smuggling goods into the United States) (20 years);
-18 U.S.C. 549 (removing goods from Customs custody) (10 years);
-18 U.S.C. 641 (public money, property, or records) (various from 1 to 10 years);
-18 U.S.C. 656 (theft, embezzlement, or misapplication by bank officer or employee) (various from 1 to 30 years);
-18 U.S.C. 657 (lending, credit, and insurance institutions) (various from 1 to 30 years);
-18 U.S.C. 658 (property mortgaged or pledged to farm credit agencies) (various from 1 to 5 years);
-18 U.S.C. 659 (felonious theft from interstate shipment) (various from 3 to 10 years);*
-18 U.S.C. 664 (embezzlement from pension and welfare funds) (various from 1 to 10 years);
-18 U.S.C. 666 (theft or bribery concerning programs receiving Federal funds) (10 years);
-18 U.S.C. 669 (federal health care offense) (various from 1 to 10 years);~
-18 U.S.C. 793, 794, 798 (espionage) (various from 1 year to life);
-18 U.S.C. 831 (prohibited transactions involving nuclear materials) (various from 10 years to life);
-18 U.S.C. 832 (participation in foreign nuclear weapons programs) (various from 20 years to life);**
-18 U.S.C. 842(m), (n) (plastic explosives) (10 years);**
-18 U.S.C. 844(f), (i) (destruction by explosives or fire of Government property or property affecting interstate or foreign commerce) (various from 20 years to life);
-18 U.S.C. 875 (interstate communications) (various from 2 to 20 years);
-18 U.S.C. 891-894 (extortionate credit transactions) (20 years);*
-18 U.S.C. 922(1) (unlawful importation of firearms) (5 years);
-18 U.S.C. 924(n) (firearms trafficking) (10 years);
-18 U.S.C. 930(c) (killing or attempted killing during an attack on a Federal facility with a dangerous weapon) (various from 7 years to life);**
-18 U.S.C. 956 (conspiracy to kill, kidnap, maim, or injure certain property in a foreign country) (various from 35 years to life);

-18 U.S.C. 1001 (false statement relating federal health care) (5 years); ~
-18 U.S.C. 1005 (fraudulent bank entries) (30 years);
-18 U.S.C. 1006 (fraudulent Federal credit institution entries) (30 years);
-18 U.S.C. 1007 (fraudulent Federal Deposit Insurance transactions) (30 years);
-18 U.S.C. 1014 (fraudulent loan or credit applications) (30 years);
-18 U.S.C. 1028 (fraud and related activity in connection with identification documents) (various from 1 to 30 years);*
-18 U.S.C. 1029 (fraud and related activity in connection with access devices) (various from 10 to 20 years);*
-18 U.S.C. 1030 (computer fraud and abuse) (various from 1 to 20 years);
-18 U.S.C. 1032 (concealment of assets from conservator, receiver, or liquidating agent of financial institution) (5 years);
-18 U.S.C. 1035 (false statements relating to federal health care) (5 years); ~
-18 U.S.C. 1084 (transmission of gambling information) (2 years);*
-18 U.S.C. 1111 (murder) (life);
-18 U.S.C. 1114 (killing a United States employee or officer) (various from 8 years to life);
-18 U.S.C. 1116 (killing a foreign official, official guest, or internationally protected person) (various from 7 years to life);
-18 U.S.C. 1201 (kidnapping) (life);
-18 U.S.C. 1203 (hostage taking) (life);
-18 U.S.C. 1341 (mail fraud) (various from 20 to 30 years);*
-18 U.S.C. 1343 (wire fraud) (various from 20 to 30 years);*
-18 U.S.C. 1344 (financial institution fraud) (30 years);*
-18 U.S.C. 1347 (federal health care fraud) (various from 20 years to life);
-18 U.S.C. 1361 (willful injury of Government property) (various from 1 to 10 years);
-18 U.S.C. 1362 (destruction of communication lines, stations, or systems) (10 years);**
-18 U.S.C. 1363 (destruction of property within the special maritime and territorial jurisdiction) (various from 5 to 20 years);
-18 U.S.C. 1366(a) (destruction of an energy facility) (20 years);**
-18 U.S.C. 1425 (procurement of citizenship or nationalization unlawfully) (various from 10 to 25 years);*
-18 U.S.C. 1426 (reproduction of naturalization or citizenship papers) (various from 10 to 25 years);*
-18 U.S.C. 1427 (sale of naturalization or citizenship papers) (various from 10 to 25 years);*

-18 U.S.C. 1461-1465 (obscene matter) (various from 2 to 10 years);*
-18 U.S.C. 1503 (obstruction of justice) (various from 8 years to life);*
-18 U.S.C. 1510 (relating to obstruction of criminal investigations) (5 years);*
-18 U.S.C. 1511 (obstruction of State or local law enforcement) (5 years);*
-18 U.S.C. 1512 (tampering with a witness, victim, or an informant) (various from 3 years to life);*
-18 U.S.C. 1513 (retaliating against a witness, victim, or an informant) (various from 8 years to life);*
-18 U.S.C. 1518 (obstructing a federal health care investigation) (5 years); ~
-18 U.S.C. 1542 (false statement in application and use of passport) (various from 10 to 25 years);*
-18 U.S.C. 1543 (forgery or false use of passport) (various from 10 to 25 years);*
-18 U.S.C. 1544 (misuse of passport) (various from 10 to 25 years);*
-18 U.S.C. 1546 (fraud and misuse of visas, permits, and other documents) (various from 10 to 25 years);*
-18 U.S.C. 1581-1592 (peonage, slavery, and trafficking in persons) (various from 2 years to life);*
-18 U.S.C. 1708 (theft from the mail) (5 years);
-18 U.S.C. 1751 (violence against the President) (various from 1 year to life);
-18 U.S.C. 1951 (interference with commerce, robbery, or extortion) (20 years);*
-18 U.S.C. 1952 (racketeering (Travel Act)) (various from 5 years to life);*
-18 U.S.C. 1953 (interstate transportation of wagering paraphernalia) (5 years);*
-18 U.S.C. 1954 (unlawful welfare fund payments) (3 years);*
-18 U.S.C. 1955 (illegal gambling businesses) (5 years);*
-18 U.S.C. 1956 (laundering of monetary instruments) (20 years);*
-18 U.S.C. 1957 (engaging in monetary transactions in property derived from specified unlawful activity) (10 years);*
-18 U.S.C. 1958 (use of interstate commerce facilities in the commission of murder-for-hire) (various from 10 years to life);*
-18 U.S.C. 1960 (money transmitters) (5 years);*
-18 U.S.C. 1992 (attacks and other acts of violence against mass transportation systems) (various from 20 years to life);**
-18 U.S.C. 2113, 2114 (bank and postal robbery and theft) (various from 1 year to life);
-18 U.S.C. 2155 (destruction of national defense materials, premises, or utilities) (various from 20 years to life);**

-18 U.S.C. 2156 (national defense material, premises, or utilities) (10 years);**
-18 U.S.C. 2251, 2251A, 2252, and 2260 (sexual exploitation of children) (various from 10 years to life);*
-18 U.S.C. 2280 (violence against maritime navigation) (various from 20 years to life);
-18 U.S.C. 2281 (violence against maritime fixed platforms) (various from 20 years to life);
-18 U.S.C. 2312, 2313 (interstate transportation of stolen motor vehicles) (10 years);*
-18 U.S.C. 2314, 2315 (interstate transportation of stolen property) (10 years)
-18 U.S.C. 2318 (trafficking in counterfeit labels for phonorecords, computer programs or computer program documentation or packaging and copies of motion pictures or other audiovisual works) (5 years);*
-18 U.S.C. 2319 (criminal infringement of a copyright) (various from 1 to 5 years);*
-18 U.S.C. 2319A (relating to unauthorized fixation of and trafficking in sound recordings and music videos of live musical performances) (various from 5 to 10 years);*
-18 U.S.C. 2320 (trafficking in goods or services bearing counterfeit marks) (various from 10 to 20 years);*
-18 U.S.C. 2321 (trafficking in certain motor vehicles or motor vehicle parts) (10 years);*
-18 U.S.C. 2332 (terrorist acts abroad against United States nationals) (various from 3 years to life);
-18 U.S.C. 2332a (use of weapons of mass destruction) (life);
-18 U.S.C. 2332b (international terrorist acts transcending national boundaries) (various from 10 years to life);
-18 U.S.C. 2332f (bombing of public places and facilities) (life);**
-18 U.S.C. 2332g (missile systems designed to destroy aircraft) (life);
-18 U.S.C. 2332h (radiological dispersal devices) (life);
-18 U.S.C. 2339 (harboring terrorists) (10 years);**
-18 U.S.C. 2339A, 2339B (providing material support to terrorists) (various from 15 years to life);
-18 U.S.C. 2339C (financing of terrorism) (various from 10 to 20 years);**
-18 U.S.C. 2339D (foreign military training) (10 years)**
-18 U.S.C. 2340A (torture) (various from 20 years to life);
-18 U.S.C. 2341-2346 (trafficking in contraband cigarettes) (various from 3 to 5 years);*

-18 U.S.C. 2421-2424 (white slave traffic) (various from 10 years to life);*
-19 U.S.C. 1590 (aviation smuggling) (various from 5 to 20 years);
-21 U.S.C. 841 et seq. (felonious manufacture, importation, receiving, concealment, buying, selling, or otherwise dealing in a controlled substance or listed chemical) (various from 1 year to life);*
-21 U.S.C. 863 (drug paraphernalia) (3 years);
-21 U.S.C. 960A (narc-terrorism) (various from 2 years to life);**
-22 U.S.C. 2778(c) (Arms Export Control Act) (10 years);
-22 U.S.C. 611 et seq. (Foreign Agents Registration Act of 1938 felony) (various from 1 to 5 years);
-29 U.S.C. 186 (dealing with restrictions on payments and loans to labor organizations) (various from 1 to 5 years);*
-29 U.S.C. 501(c) (embezzlement from union funds) (5 years);*
-33 U.S.C. 1251 et seq. (Federal Water Pollution Control Act felony) (various from 1 to 15 years);
-33 U.S.C. 1401 et seq. (Ocean Dumping Act felony) (5 years);
-33 U.S.C. 1901 et seq. (Act to Prevent Pollution from Ships felony) (6 years);
-42 U.S.C. 300f et seq. (Safe Drinking Water Act felony) (various from 3 to 20 years);
-42 U.S.C. 1490s(a)(1) (Housing Act of 1949 (equity skimming)) (5 years);
-42 U.S.C. 2122 (atomic weapons) (life);
-42 U.S.C. 2284 (sabotage of nuclear facilities or fuel) (various from 20 years to life);**
-42 U.S.C. 6901 et seq. (Resources Conservation and Recovery Act felony) (various from 2 to 15 years);
-49 U.S.C. 46502 of title 49 (air piracy) (life);
-49 U.S.C. 46504 (second sentence) (relating to assault on a flight crew with a dangerous weapon) (various from 20 years to life);**
-49 U.S.C. 46505(b)(3), (c) (explosive or incendiary devices, or endangerment of human life by means of weapons, on aircraft) (various from 10 to 20 years);**
-49 U.S.C. 46506 (if homicide or attempted homicide is involved) (application of certain criminal laws to acts on aircraft) (various from 7 years to life);**
-49 U.S.C. 60123(b) (destruction of interstate gas or hazardous liquid pipeline facility) (various from 5 years to life);**
-50 U.S.C. 1705 (International Emergency Economic Powers Act) (20 years);
-50 U.S.C. App. 16 (Trading with the Enemy Act) (10 years).

STATE MONEY LAUNDERING LAWS (CITATIONS)

Arizona: Ariz. Rev. Stat. Ann. §13-2317
Arkansas: Ark .Code Ann. §§5-42-201 to 5-42-205
California: Cal. Penal Code §§186.9, 186.10
Colorado: Colo. Rev. Stat. Ann. §18-18-408
Connecticut: Conn. Gen. Stat. Ann. §§53a-275 to 53a-282
Delaware: Del. Code Ann. tit. 11, §951
Florida: Fla. Stat. Ann.§§896.101 to 896.107
Georgia: GA. CODE §§7-1-910 to 7-1-916
Hawaii: HAWAII REV. STAT. §§708A-1 to 708A-3
Idaho: IDAHO CODE §18-8201
Illinois: ILL. COMP. LAWS ANN. ch.720 §5/29B-1
Indiana: IND. CODE ANN. §§35-45-15-1 to 35-45-15-5
Iowa: IOWA CODE ANN. §§706B.1 to 706B.3
Kansas: KAN. STAT. ANN. §65-4142
Louisiana: LA. REV. STAT. ANN. §14:230
Michigan: Mich. Comp. Laws Ann. §§750.411j to 750.411p
Mississippi: Miss. Code Ann. §97-23-101
Missouri: Mo. Ann. Stat. §574.105
Montana: Mont. Code Ann. §45-6-341
Nebraska: Neb. Rev. Stat. §28-205
New Jersey: N.J. Stat. Ann. §§2C:21-23 to 2C:21-29
New Mexico: N.Mex. Stat. Ann. §§30-51-1 to 30-51-5
New York: N.Y. Penal Law §§470.00 to 470.25
North Dakota: N.D. Cent. Code §19-03.1-23, 12.1- 08-04
Ohio: OHIO REV. CODE ANN. §§ 1315.55, 2909.29
Oklahoma: OKLA. STAT. ANN., tit.21 §2001
Oregon: ORE. REV. STAT. §§164.170 to 164.174
Pennsylvania: 18 PA. CONS. STAT. ANN. §5111
Rhode Island: R.I. GEN. LAWS §11-9.1-15
South Carolina: S.C. CODE ANN. §44-53-475
Tennessee: TENN. CODE ANN. §§39-14-901 to 39-14- 909
Texas: TEX. PENAL CODE ANN. §§34.01 to 34.03
Utah: UTAH CODE ANN. §§76-10-1901 to 76-10-1908
Virginia: VA. CODE ANN. §§18.2-246.1 to 18.2-246.5
Washington: WASH. REV. CODE ANN. §§9A.83.010 to 9A.83.04

State Money Transmission Laws (Citations)

Alabama: Ala. Code §§5-22-1 to 5-22-8
Alaska: Alaska Stat. §§06.55.101 to 06.55.995
Arizona: Ariz. Rev. Stat. Ann. §§6-1201 to 6-1219
Arkansas: Ark. Code Ann. §§23-55-101 to 23-55-1005
California: Cal. Fin. Code §§1800 to 1827
Connecticut: Conn. Gen. Stat. Ann. §§36a-595 to 36a610
Colorado: Colo. Rev. Stat. Ann. §§12-52-101 to 12-52- 117
Delaware: Del. Code Ann. tit.5 §§2301 to 2318
District of Columbia: D.C. Code §§26-1001 to 26- 1026
Florida: Fla.Stat.Ann.§§560.101 to 560.408, 655.50
Georgia: Ga. Code Ann. §§7-1-680 to 7-1-692
Hawaii: Haw. Rev. Stat. §§4889D-1 to 489D-34
Idaho: Idaho Code §§26-2901 to 26-2928
Illinois: Ill. Comp. Laws Ann. ch.205 §§657/1 to 657/105
Indiana: Ind. Code Ann. §§28-8-4-1 to 28-8-4-61
Iowa: IOWA CODE ANN. §§533C.201 to 533C.904
Kansas: Kan. Stat. Ann. §§9-50 to 9-513d
Kentucky: KY. REV. STAT. ANN. §§286.11.001 TO 286.11.067
Louisiana: La. Rev. Stat. Ann. §§6:1301 to 6:1054
Maine: ME. REV. STAT. ANN. tit. 32 §§6101 to 6162
Maryland: Md. Fin. Inst. Code §§12-401 to 12-431
Massachusetts: MASS. GEN. LAWS ANN. ch.169 §§1 to 16
Michigan: MICH. COMP. LAWS §§487.1001 TO 487.1047
MINNESOTA: MINN. STAT. ANN. §§53B.01 TO 53B.26
Nevada: NEV. REV. STAT §§671.010 TO 671.190
New Hampshire: N.H. Rev. Stat. Ann. §§399-G:1 to 399- G:22
New Jersey: N.J. Stat. Ann. §§17:15C-1 to 17:15C-27
New York: New York Banking Law §§640 to 652-b
North Carolina: N.C. Gen. Stat. §§53-208.1 to 208.30
North Dakota: N.D. Cent. Code §§13-09-01 to 13-09-24
Ohio: Ohio Rev. Code Ann. §§1315.01 to 1315.99
Oklahoma: Okla. Stat. Ann. tit. 6 §§1511 to 1515
Oregon: Ore. Rev. Stat. §§717.200 to 717.905
Pennsylvania :Pa. Stat. Ann. tit.7 §§6101 to 6118
South Dakota: S.D. Codified Laws §§51A-17-1 to 51A17-47

Tennessee: TENN. CODE ANN. §§45-7-201 to 45-7-226
Texas: TEX. FIN. CODE ANN. §§151.301 to 151.405
Vermont: VT. STAT. ANN. tit.8 §§2501 to 2555
Virginia: VA. CODE ANN. §§6.1-370 to 6.1-378.4
Washington: WASH. REV. CODE ANN. §§19.230.005 to 19.230.905
West Virginia: W.VA. CODE ANN. §§32A-2-1 to 32A-2-28
Wyoming: WYO. STAT. §§40-22-101 to 40-22-129

Selected Federal Money Laundering Laws (Text)

18 U.S.C. 1956. Laundering of monetary instruments

(a)(1) Whoever, knowing that the property involved in a financial transaction represents the proceeds of some form of unlawful activity, conducts or attempts to conduct such a financial transaction which in fact involves the proceeds of specified unlawful activity–

(A)(i) with the intent to promote the carrying on of specified unlawful activity; or

(ii) with intent to engage in conduct constituting a violation of section 7201 or 7206 of the Internal Revenue Code of 1986; or

(B) knowing that the transaction is designed in whole or in part–

(i) to conceal or disguise the nature, the location, the source, the ownership, or the control of the proceeds of specified unlawful activity; or

(ii) to avoid a transaction reporting requirement under State or Federal law, shall be sentenced to a fine of not more than $500,000 or twice the value of the property involved in the transaction, whichever is greater, or imprisonment for not more than twenty years, or both. For purposes of this paragraph, a financial transaction shall be considered to be one involving the proceeds of specified unlawful activity if it is part of a set of parallel or dependent transactions, any one of which involves the proceeds of specified unlawful activity, and all of which are part of a single plan or arrangement.

(2) Whoever transports, transmits, or transfers, or attempts to transport, transmit, or transfer a monetary instrument or funds from a place in the United States to or through a place outside the United States or to a place in the United States from or through a place outside the United States–

(A) with the intent to promote the carrying on of specified unlawful activity; or

(B) knowing that the monetary instrument or funds involved in the transportation, transmission, or transfer represent the proceeds of some form of unlawful activity and knowing that such transportation, transmission, or transfer is designed in whole or in part–

(i) to conceal or disguise the nature, the location, the source, the ownership, or the control of the proceeds of specified unlawful activity; or

(ii) to avoid a transaction reporting requirement under State or Federal law, shall be sentenced to a fine of not more than $500,000 or twice the value of the monetary instrument or funds involved in the transportation, transmission, or transfer whichever is greater, or imprisonment for not more than twenty years, or both.

For the purpose of the offense described in subparagraph (B), the defendant's knowledge may be established by proof that a law enforcement officer represented the matter specified in subparagraph (B) as true, and the defendant's subsequent statements or actions indicate that the defendant believed such representations to be true.

(3) Whoever, with the intent–

(A) to promote the carrying on of specified unlawful activity;

(B) to conceal or disguise the nature, location, source, ownership, or control of property believed to be the proceeds of specified unlawful activity; or

(C) to avoid a transaction reporting requirement under State or Federal law, conducts or attempts to conduct a financial transaction involving property represented to be the proceeds of specified unlawful activity, or property used to conduct or facilitate specified unlawful activity, shall be fined under this title or imprisoned for not more than 20 years, or both. For purposes of this paragraph and paragraph (2), the term "represented" means any representation made by a law enforcement officer or by another person at the direction of, or with the approval of, a Federal official authorized to investigate or prosecute violations of this section.

(b) Penalties.–

(1) In general.– Whoever conducts or attempts to conduct a transaction described in subsection (a)(1) or (a)(3), or section 1957, or a transportation, transmission, or transfer described in subsection (a)(2), is liable to the United States for a civil penalty of not more than the greater of–

(A) the value of the property, funds, or monetary instruments involved in the transaction; or

(B) $10,000.

(2) Jurisdiction over foreign persons.– For purposes of adjudicating an action filed or enforcing a penalty ordered under this section, the district courts shall have jurisdiction over any foreign person, including any financial institution authorized under the laws of a foreign country, against whom the action is brought, if service of process upon the foreign person is made under the Federal Rules of Civil Procedure or the laws of the country in which the foreign person is found, and–

(A) the foreign person commits an offense under subsection (a) involving a financial transaction that occurs in whole or in part in the United States;

(B) the foreign person converts, to his or her own use, property in which the United States has an ownership interest by virtue of the entry of an order of forfeiture by a court of the United States; or

(C) the foreign person is a financial institution that maintains a bank account at a financial institution in the United States.

(3) Court authority over assets.– A court may issue a pretrial restraining order or take any other action necessary to ensure that any bank account or other property held by the defendant in the United States is available to satisfy a judgment under this section.

(4) Federal receiver.–

(A) In general.–A court may appoint a Federal Receiver, in accordance with subparagraph (B) of this paragraph, to collect, marshal, and take custody, control, and possession of all assets of the defendant, wherever located, to satisfy a civil judgment under this subsection, a forfeiture judgment under section 981 or 982, or a criminal sentence under section 1957 or subsection (a) of this section, including an order of restitution to any victim of a specified unlawful activity.

(B) Appointment and authority.–A Federal Receiver described in subparagraph (A)–

(i) may be appointed upon application of a Federal prosecutor or a Federal or State regulator, by the court having jurisdiction over the defendant in the case;

(ii) shall be an officer of the court, and the powers of the Federal Receiver shall include the powers set out in section 754 of title 28, United States Code; and shall have standing equivalent to that of a Federal prosecutor for the purpose of submitting requests to obtain information regarding the assets of the defendant–

(I) from the Financial Crimes Enforcement Network of the Department of the Treasury; or

(II) from a foreign country pursuant to a mutual legal assistance treaty, multilateral agreement, or other arrangement for international law enforcement assistance, provided that such requests are in accordance with the policies and procedures of the Attorney General.

(c) As used in this section–

(1) the term "knowing that the property involved in a financial transaction represents the proceeds of some form of unlawful activity" means that the person knew the property involved in the transaction represented proceeds from some form, though not necessarily which form, of activity that constitutes a felony under State, Federal, or foreign law, regardless of whether or not such activity is specified in paragraph (7);

(2) the term "conducts" includes initiating, concluding, or participating in initiating, or concluding a transaction;

(3) the term "transaction" includes a purchase, sale, loan, pledge, gift, transfer, delivery, or other disposition, and with respect to a financial institution includes a deposit, withdrawal, transfer between accounts, exchange of currency, loan, extension of credit, purchase or sale of any stock, bond, certificate of deposit, or other monetary instrument, use of a safe deposit box, or any other payment, transfer, or delivery by, through, or to a financial institution, by whatever means effected;

(4) the term "financial transaction" means

(A) a transaction which in any way or degree affects interstate or foreign commerce

(i) involving the movement of funds by wire or other means or

(ii) involving one or more monetary instruments, or

(iii) involving the transfer of title to any real property, vehicle, vessel, or aircraft, or

(B) a transaction involving the use of a financial institution which is engaged in, or the activities of which affect, interstate or foreign commerce in any way or degree;

(5) the term "monetary instruments" means (i) coin or currency of the United States or of any other country, travelers' checks, personal checks, bank checks, and money orders, or (ii) investment securities or negotiable instruments, in bearer form or otherwise in such form that title thereto passes upon delivery;

(6) the term "financial institution" includes–

(A) any financial institution, as defined in section 5312(a)(2) of title 31, United States Code, or the regulations promulgated thereunder; and

(B) any foreign bank, as defined in section 1 of the International Banking Act of 1978 (12 U.S.C. 3101);

(7) the term "specified unlawful activity" means–

(A) any act or activity constituting an offense listed in section 1961(1) of this title except an act which is indictable under subchapter II of chapter 53 of title 31;

(B) with respect to a financial transaction occurring in whole or in part in the United States, an offense against a foreign nation involving–

(i) the manufacture, importation, sale, or distribution of a controlled substance (as such term is defined for the purposes of the Controlled Substances Act);

(ii) murder, kidnapping, robbery, extortion, destruction of property by means of explosive or fire, or a crime of violence (as defined in section 16);

(iii) fraud, or any scheme or attempt to defraud, by or against a foreign bank (as defined in paragraph 7 of section 1(b) of the International Banking Act of 1978);

(iv) bribery of a public official, or the misappropriation, theft, or embezzlement of public funds by or for the benefit of a public official;

(v) smuggling or export control violations involving–

(I) an item controlled on the United States Munitions List established under section 38 of the Arms Export Control Act (22 U.S.C. 2778); or

(II) an item controlled under regulations under the Export Administration Regulations (15 C.F.R. Parts 730-774);

(vi) an offense with respect to which the United States would be obligated by a multilateral treaty, either to extradite the alleged offender or to submit the case for prosecution, if the offender were found within the territory of the United States; or

(vii) trafficking in persons, selling or buying children, sexual exploitation of children, or transporting, recruiting or harboring a person, including a child, for commercial sex acts;

(C) any act or acts constituting a continuing criminal enterprise, as that term is defined in section 408 of the Controlled Substances Act (21 U.S.C. 848);

(D) an offense under section 32 (relating to the destruction of aircraft), section 37 (relating to violence at international airports), section 115 (relating to influencing, impeding, or retaliating against a Federal official by threatening or injuring a family member), section 152 (relating to concealment of assets; false oaths and claims; bribery), section 215 (relating to commissions or gifts for procuring loans), section 351 (relating to congressional or Cabinet officer assassination), any of sections 500 through 503 (relating to certain counterfeiting offenses), section 513 (relating to securities of States and private entities), section 541 (relating to goods falsely classified), section 542 (relating to entry of goods by means of false statements), section 545 (relating to smuggling goods into the United States), section 549 (relating to removing goods from Customs custody), section 544 (relating to smuggling goods from the United States), section 641 (relating to public money, property, or records), section 656 (relating to theft, embezzlement, or misapplication by bank officer or employee), section 657 (relating to lending, credit, and insurance institutions), section 658 (relating to property mortgaged or pledged to farm credit agencies), section 666 (relating to theft or bribery concerning programs receiving Federal funds), section 793, 794, or 798 (relating to espionage), section 831 (relating to prohibited transactions involving nuclear materials), section 844(f) or (i) (relating to destruction by explosives or fire of Government property or property affecting interstate or foreign commerce), section 875 (relating to interstate communications), section 922(1) (relating to the unlawful importation of firearms), section 924(n) (relating to firearms trafficking), section 956 (relating to conspiracy to kill, kidnap, maim, or injure certain property in a foreign country), section 1005 (relating to fraudulent bank entries), 1006 (relating to fraudulent Federal credit institution entries), 1007 (relating to fraudulent Federal Deposit Insurance transactions), 1014 (relating to fraudulent loan or credit applications), section 1030 (relating to computer fraud and abuse), 1032 (relating to concealment of assets from conservator, receiver, or liquidating agent of financial institution), section 1111 (relating to murder), section 1114 (relating to murder of United States law enforcement officials), section 1116 (relating to murder of foreign officials, official guests, or internationally protected persons), section 1201 (relating to kidnapping), section 1203 (relating to hostage taking), section 1361 (relating to willful injury of Government property), section 1363 (relating to destruction of property within the special maritime and territorial jurisdiction), section 1708 (theft from the mail), section 1751 (relating to Presidential assassination), section 2113 or 2114 (relating to bank and postal robbery and theft), section 2252A (relating to child pornography) where the child pornography contains a visual depiction of an actual minor engaging in sexually explicit conduct, section 2260 (production of certain child pornography for importation into the United States), section 2280 (relating to violence against maritime navigation), section 2281 (relating to violence against maritime fixed platforms), section 2319 (relating to copyright infringement), section 2320 (relating to trafficking in counterfeit goods and services), section 2332 (relating to terrorist acts abroad against United States nationals), section 2332a (relating to use of weapons of mass destruction), section 2332b (relating to international terrorist acts transcending national boundaries), section 2339A or 2339B (relating to providing material support to terrorists), section 2339C (relating to financing of terrorism), or section 2339D (relating to receiving military-type training from a foreign terrorist organization) of this title, section 46502 of title 49, United States Code, a felony violation of the Chemical Diversion and Trafficking Act of 1988 (relating to precursor and essential chemicals), section 590 of the Tariff Act of 1930 (19 U.S.C. 1590) (relating to aviation smuggling), section 422 of the Controlled Substances Act (relating to transportation of drug paraphernalia), section 38(c) (relating to criminal violations) of the Arms Export Control Act, section 11 (relating to violations) of the Export Administration Act of 1979, section 206 (relating to penalties) of the International Emergency Economic Powers Act, section 16 (relating to offenses and punishment) of the Trading with the Enemy Act, any felony violation of section 15 of the Food Stamp Act of 1977 [7 U.S.C.A. 2024] (relating to supplemental nutrition assistance program benefits fraud) involving a quantity of benefits having a value of not less than $5,000, any violation of section 543(a)(1) of the Housing Act of 1949 [42 U.S.C. 1490s(a)(1)] (relating to equity skimming), any felony violation of the Foreign Agents Registration Act of 1938, or any felony violation of the Foreign Corrupt Practices Act;

(E) a felony violation of the Federal Water Pollution Control Act (33 U.S.C. 1251 et seq.), the Ocean Dumping Act (33 U.S.C. 1401 et seq.), the Act to Prevent Pollution from Ships (33 U.S.C. 1901 et seq.), the Safe Drinking Water Act (42 U.S.C. 300f et seq.), or the Resources Conservation and Recovery Act (42 U.S.C. 6901 et seq.); or

(F) any act or activity constituting an offense involving a Federal health care offense;

(8) he term "State" includes a State of the United States, the District of Columbia, and any commonwealth, territory, or possession of the United States; and

(9) the term "proceeds" means any property derived from or obtained or retained, directly or indirectly, through some form of unlawful activity, including the gross receipts of such activity.

(d) Nothing in this section shall supersede any provision of Federal, State, or other law imposing criminal penalties or affording civil remedies in addition to those provided for in this section.

(e) Violations of this section may be investigated by such components of the Department of Justice as the Attorney General may direct, and by such components of the Department of the Treasury as the Secretary of the Treasury may direct, as appropriate, and, with respect to offenses over which the Department of Homeland Security has jurisdiction, by such components of the Department of Homeland Security as the Secretary of Homeland Security may direct, and, with respect to offenses over which the United States Postal Service has jurisdiction, by the Postal Service. Such authority of the Secretary of the Treasury, the Secretary of Homeland Security, and the Postal Service shall be exercised in accordance with an agreement which shall be entered into by the Secretary of the Treasury, the Secretary of Homeland Security, the Postal Service, and the Attorney General.

Violations of this section involving offenses described in paragraph (c)(7)(E) may be investigated by such components of the Department of Justice as the Attorney General may direct, and the National Enforcement Investigations Center of the Environmental Protection Agency.

(f) There is extraterritorial jurisdiction over the conduct prohibited by this section if–

(1) the conduct is by a United States citizen or, in the case of a non-United States citizen, the conduct occurs in part in the United States; and

(2) the transaction or series of related transactions involves funds or monetary instruments of a value exceeding $10,000.

(g) Notice of conviction of financial institutions.–If any financial institution or any officer, director, or employee of any financial institution has been found guilty of an offense under this section, section 1957 or 1960 of this title, or section 5322 or 5324 of title 31, the Attorney General shall provide written notice of such fact to the appropriate regulatory agency for the financial institution.

(h) Any person who conspires to commit any offense defined in this section or section 1957 shall be subject to the same penalties as those prescribed for the offense the commission of which was the object of the conspiracy.

(i) Venue.–

(1) Except as provided in paragraph (2), a prosecution for an offense under this section or section 1957 may be brought in–

(A) any district in which the financial or monetary transaction is conducted; or

(B) any district where a prosecution for the underlying specified unlawful activity could be brought, if the defendant participated in the transfer of the proceeds of the specified unlawful activity from that district to the district where the financial or monetary transaction is conducted.

(2) A prosecution for an attempt or conspiracy offense under this section or section 1957 may be brought in the district where venue would lie for the completed offense under paragraph (1), or in any other district where an act in furtherance of the attempt or conspiracy took place.

(3) For purposes of this section, a transfer of funds from 1 place to another, by wire or any other means, shall constitute a single, continuing transaction. Any person who conducts (as that term is defined in subsection (c)(2)) any portion of the transaction may be charged in any district in which the transaction takes place.

18 U.S.C. 1956 Note. [P.L. 111-21, Sec. 2(G)]. Sense of the Congress and Report Concerning Required Approval for Merger Cases

(1) Sense of Congress. – It is the sense of the Congress that no prosecution of an offense under section 1956 or 1957 of title 18, United States Code, should be undertaken in combination with the prosecution of any other offense, without prior approval of the Attorney General, the Deputy Attorney General, the Assistant Attorney General in charge of the Criminal Division, a Deputy Assistant Attorney General in the Criminal Division, or the relevant United States Attorney, if the conduct to be charged as "specified unlawful activity" in connection with the offense under section 1956 or 1957 is so closely connected with the conduct to be charged as the other offense that there is no clear delineation between the two offenses.

(2) Report. – One year after the date of the enactment of this Act, and at the end of each of the four succeeding one-year periods, the Attorney General shall report to the House and Senate Committees on the Judiciary on efforts undertaken by the Department of Justice to ensure the review and approval described in paragraph (1) takes place in all appropriate cases.

The report shall include the following:

(A) The number of prosecutions described in paragraph (1) that were undertaken during the previous one-year period after prior approval by an official described in paragraph (1), classified by type of offense and by the approving official.

(B) The number of prosecutions described in paragraph (12) that were undertaken during the previous one-year period without such prior approval, classified by type of offense, and the reasons why such prior approval was not obtained.

(C) The number of times during the previous year in which an approval described in paragraph (1) was denied.

18 U.S.C. 1957. Engaging in Monetary Transactions in Property Derived from Specified Unlawful Activity

(a) Whoever, in any of the circumstances set forth in subsection (d), knowingly engages or attempts to engage in a monetary transaction in criminally derived property that is of a value greater than $10,000 and is derived from specified unlawful activity, shall be punished as provided in subsection (b).

(b)(1) Except as provided in paragraph (2), the punishment for an offense under this section is a fine under title 18, United States Code, or imprisonment for not more than ten years or both.

(2) The court may impose an alternate fine to that imposable under paragraph (1) of not more than twice the amount of the criminally derived property involved in the transaction.

(c) In a prosecution for an offense under this section, the Government is not required to prove the defendant knew that the offense from which the criminally derived property was derived was specified unlawful activity.

(d) The circumstances referred to in subsection (a) are –

(1) that the offense under this section takes place in the United States or in the special maritime and territorial jurisdiction of the United States; or

(2) that the offense under this section takes place outside the United States and such special jurisdiction, but the defendant is a United States person (as defined in section 3077 of this title, but excluding the class described in paragraph (2)(D) of such section).

(e) Violations of this section may be investigated by such components of the Department of Justice as the Attorney General may direct, and by such components of the Department of the Treasury as the Secretary of the Treasury may direct, as appropriate, and, with respect to offenses over which the Department of Homeland Security has jurisdiction, by such components of the Department of Homeland Security as the Secretary of Homeland Security may direct, and, with respect to offenses over which the United States Postal Service has jurisdiction, by the Postal Service. Such authority of the Secretary of the Treasury, the Secretary of Homeland Security, and the Postal Service shall be exercised in accordance with an agreement which shall be entered into by the Secretary of the Treasury, the Secretary of Homeland Security, the Postal Service, and the Attorney General.

(f) As used in this section–

(1) the term "monetary transaction" means the deposit, withdrawal, transfer, or exchange, in or affecting interstate or foreign commerce, of funds or a monetary instrument (as defined in section 1956(c)(5) of this title) by, through, or to a financial institution (as defined in section 1956 of this title), including any transaction that would be a financial transaction under section 1956(c)(4)(B) of this title, but such term does not include any transaction necessary to preserve a person's right to representation as guaranteed by the sixth amendment to the Constitution;

(2) the term "criminally derived property" means any property constituting, or derived from, proceeds obtained from a criminal offense; and

(3) the term "specified unlawful activity" and "proceeds" shall have the meaning given that term in section 1956 of this title.

Travel Act: 18 U.S.C. 1952. Interstate and Foreign Travel or Transportation in Aid of Racketeering Enterprises

(a) Whoever travels in interstate or foreign commerce or uses the mail or any facility in interstate or foreign commerce, with intent to–

(1) distribute the proceeds of any unlawful activity; or

(2) commit any crime of violence to further any unlawful activity; or

(3) otherwise promote, manage, establish, carry on, or facilitate the promotion, management, establishment, or carrying on, of any unlawful activity, and thereafter performs or attempts to perform–

(A) an act described in paragraph (1) or (3) shall be fined under this title, imprisoned not more than five years, or both; or

(B) an act described in paragraph (2) shall be fined under this title, imprisoned for not more than 20 years, or both, and if death results shall be imprisoned for any term of years or for life.

(b) As used in this section (i) "unlawful activity" means

(1) any business enterprise involving gambling, liquor on which the Federal excise tax has not been paid, narcotics or controlled substances (as defined in section 102(6) of the Controlled Substances Act), or prostitution offenses in violation of the laws of the State in which they are committed or of the United States,

(2) extortion, bribery, or arson in violation of the laws of the State in which committed or of the United States, or
(3) any act which is indictable under subchapter II of chapter 53 of title 31, United States Code, or under section 1956 or 1957 of this title and (ii) the term "State" includes a State of the United States, the District of Columbia, and any commonwealth, territory, or possession of the United States.
(c) Investigations of violations under this section involving liquor shall be conducted under the supervision of the Attorney General.

31 U.S.C. 5322: Reporting Requirements

(a) A person willfully violating this subchapter or a regulation prescribed or order issued under this subchapter (except section 5315 or 5324 of this title or a regulation prescribed under section 5315 or 5324), or willfully violating a regulation prescribed under section 21 of the Federal Deposit Insurance Act or section 123 of Public Law 91-508, shall be fined not more than $250,000, or imprisoned for not more than five years, or both.
(b) A person willfully violating this subchapter or a regulation prescribed or order issued under this subchapter (except section 5315 or 5324 of this title or a regulation prescribed under section 5315 or 5324), or willfully violating a regulation prescribed under section 21 of the Federal Deposit Insurance Act or section 123 of Public Law 91-508, while violating another law of the United States or as part of a pattern of any illegal activity involving more than $100,000 in a 12-month period, shall be fined not more than $500,000, imprisoned for not more than 10 years, or both.
(c) For a violation of section 5318(a)(2) of this title or a regulation prescribed under section 5318(a)(2), a separate violation occurs for each day the violation continues and at each office, branch, or place of business at which a violation occurs or continues.
(d) A financial institution or agency that violates any provision of subsection (i) or (j) of section 5318, or any special measures imposed under section 5318A, or any regulation prescribed under subsection (i) or (j) of section 5318 or section 5318A, shall be fined in an amount equal to not less than 2 times the amount of the transaction, but not more than $1,000,000.

31 U.S.C. 5324. Structuring Transactions to Evade Reporting Requirement Prohibited

(a) Domestic coin and currency transactions involving financial institutions.– No person shall, for the purpose of evading the reporting requirements of section 5313(a) or 5325 or any regulation prescribed under any such section, the reporting or recordkeeping requirements imposed by any order issued under section 5326, or the recordkeeping requirements imposed by any regulation prescribed under section 21 of the Federal Deposit Insurance Act or section 123 of Public Law 91-508–

(1) cause or attempt to cause a domestic financial institution to fail to file a report required under section 5313(a) or 5325 or any regulation prescribed under any such section, to file a report or to maintain a record required by an order issued under section 5326, or to maintain a record required pursuant to any regulation prescribed under section 21 of the Federal Deposit Insurance Act or section 123 of Public Law 91-508;

(2) cause or attempt to cause a domestic financial institution to file a report required under section 5313(a) or 5325 or any regulation prescribed under any such section, to file a report or to maintain a record required by any order issued under section 5326, or to maintain a record required pursuant to any regulation prescribed under section 5326, or to maintain a record required pursuant to any regulation prescribed under section 21 of the Federal Deposit Insurance Act or section 123 of Public Law 91-508, that contains a material omission or misstatement of fact; or

(3) structure or assist in structuring, or attempt to structure or assist in structuring, any transaction with one or more domestic financial institutions.

(b) Domestic coin and currency transactions involving nonfinancial trades or businesses.–No person shall, for the purpose of evading the report requirements of section 5331 or any regulation prescribed under such section—

(1) cause or attempt to cause a nonfinancial trade or business to fail to file a report required under section 5331 or any regulation prescribed under such section;

(2) cause or attempt to cause a nonfinancial trade or business to file a report required under section 5331 or any regulation prescribed under such section that contains a material omission or misstatement of fact; or

(3) structure or assist in structuring, or attempt to structure or assist in structuring, any transaction with 1 or more nonfinancial trades or businesses.

(c) International monetary instrument transactions.–No person shall, for the purpose of evading the reporting requirements of section 5316 –
(1) fail to file a report required by section 5316, or cause or attempt to cause a person to fail to file such a report;
(2) file or cause or attempt to cause a person to file a report required under section 5316 that contains a material omission or misstatement of fact; or
(3) structure or assist in structuring, or attempt to structure or assist in structuring, any importation or exportation of monetary instruments.
(d) Criminal penalty.–
(1) In general.– Whoever violates this section shall be fined in accordance with title 18, United States Code, imprisoned for not more than five years, or both.
(2) Enhanced penalty for aggravated cases.– Whoever violates this section while violating another law of the United States or as part of a pattern of any illegal activity involving more than $100,000 in a 12-month period shall be fined twice the amount provided in subsection (b)(3) or (c)(3) (as the case may be) of section 3571 of title 18, United States Code, imprisoned for not more than 10 years, or both.

31 U.S.C. 5332. Bulk Cash Smuggling

(a) Criminal offense.–
(1) In general.–Whoever, with the intent to evade a currency reporting requirement under section 5316, knowingly conceals more than $10,000 in currency or other monetary instruments on the person of such individual or in any conveyance, article of luggage, merchandise, or other container, and transports or transfers or attempts to transport or transfer such currency or monetary instruments from a place within the United States to a place outside of the United States, or from a place outside the United States to a place within the United States, shall be guilty of a currency smuggling offense and subject to punishment pursuant to subsection (b).
(2) Concealment on person.–For purposes of this section, the concealment of currency on the person of any individual includes concealment in any article of clothing worn by the individual or in any luggage, backpack, or other container worn or carried by such individual.
(b) Penalty.– (1) Term of imprisonment.–A person convicted of a currency smuggling offense under subsection (a), or a conspiracy to commit such offense, shall be imprisoned for not more than five years.

(2) Forfeiture.–In addition, the court, in imposing sentence under paragraph (1), shall order that the defendant forfeit to the United States, any property, real or personal, involved in the offense, and any property traceable to such property.

(3) Procedure.–The seizure, restraint, and forfeiture of property under this section shall be governed by section 413 of the Controlled Substances Act.

(4) Personal money judgment.–If the property subject to forfeiture under paragraph (2) is unavailable, and the defendant has insufficient substitute property that may be forfeited pursuant to section 413(p) of the Controlled Substances Act, the court shall enter a personal money judgment against the defendant for the amount that would be subject to forfeiture.

(c) Civil forfeiture.–

(1) In general.–Any property involved in a violation of subsection (a), or a conspiracy to commit such violation, and any property traceable to such violation or conspiracy, may be seized and forfeited to the United States.

(2) Procedure.–The seizure and forfeiture shall be governed by the procedures governing civil forfeitures in money laundering cases pursuant to section 981(a)(1)(A) of title 18, United States Code.

(3) Treatment of certain property as involved in the offense.–For purposes of this subsection and subsection (b), any currency or other monetary instrument that is concealed or intended to be concealed in violation of subsection (a) or a conspiracy to commit such violation, any article, container, or conveyance used, or intended to be used, to conceal or transport the currency or other monetary instrument, and any other property used, or intended to be used, to facilitate the offense, shall be considered property involved in the offense.

18 U.S.C. 1960. Prohibition of Unlicensed Money Transmitting Businesses

(a) Whoever knowingly conducts, controls, manages, supervises, directs, or owns all or part of an unlicensed money transmitting business, shall be fined in accordance with this title or imprisoned not more than 5 years, or both.

(b) As used in this section –

(1) the term “unlicensed money transmitting business” means a money transmitting business which affects interstate or foreign commerce in any manner or degree and –

(A) is operated without an appropriate money transmitting license in a State where such operation is punishable as a misdemeanor or a felony under

State law, whether or not the defendant knew that the operation was required to be licensed or that the operation was so punishable;

(B) fails to comply with the money transmitting business registration requirements under section 5330 of title 31, United States Code, or regulations prescribed under such section; or

(C) otherwise involves the transportation or transmission of funds that are known to the defendant to have been derived from a criminal offense or are intended to be used to promote or support unlawful activity;

(2) the term "money transmitting" includes transferring funds on behalf of the public by any and all means including but not limited to transfers within this country or to locations abroad by wire, check, draft, facsimile, or courier; and

(3) the term "State" means any State of the United States, the District of Columbia, the Northern Mariana Islands, and any commonwealth, territory, or possession of the United States.

Rico: 18 U.S.C. 1962. Prohibited Activities

(a) It shall be unlawful for any person who has received any income derived, directly or indirectly, from a pattern of racketeering activity or through collection of an unlawful debt in which such person has participated as a principal within the meaning of section 2, title 18, United States Code, to use or invest, directly or indirectly, any part of such income, or the proceeds of such income, in acquisition of any interest in, or the establishment or operation of, any enterprise which is engaged in, or the activities of which affect, interstate or foreign commerce. A purchase of securities on the open market for purposes of investment, and without the intention of controlling or participating in the control of the issuer, or of assisting another to do so, shall not be unlawful under this subsection if the securities of the issuer held by the purchaser, the members of his immediate family, and his or their accomplices in any pattern or racketeering activity or the collection of an unlawful debt after such purchase do not amount in the aggregate to one percent of the outstanding securities of any one class, and do not confer, either in law or in fact, the power to elect one or more directors of the issuer.

(b) It shall be unlawful for any person through a pattern of racketeering activity or through collection of an unlawful debt to acquire or maintain, directly or indirectly, any interest in or control of any enterprise which is engaged in, or the activities of which affect, interstate or foreign commerce.

(c) It shall be unlawful for any person employed by or associated with any enterprise engaged in, or the activities of which affect, interstate or foreign commerce, to conduct or participate, directly or indirectly, in the conduct of such enterprise's affairs through a pattern of racketeering activity or collection of unlawful debt.

(d) It shall be unlawful for any person to conspire to violate any of the provisions of subsection (a), (b), or (c) of this section.

18 U.S.C. 1961. Definitions

As used in this chapter–

(1) "racketeering activity" means

(A) any act or threat involving murder, kidnapping, gambling, arson, robbery, bribery, extortion, dealing in obscene matter, or dealing in a controlled substance or listed chemical (as defined in section 102 of the Controlled Substances Act), which is chargeable under State law and punishable by imprisonment for more than one year;

(B) any act which is indictable under any of the following provisions of title 18, United States Code: Section 201 (relating to bribery), section 224 (relating to sports bribery), sections 471, 472, and 473 (relating to counterfeiting), section 659 (relating to theft from interstate shipment) if the act indictable under section 659 is felonious, section 664 (relating to embezzlement from pension and welfare funds), sections 891-894 (relating to extortionate credit transactions), section 1028 (relating to fraud and related activity in connection with identification documents), section 1029 (relating to fraud and related activity in connection with access devices), section 1084 (relating to the transmission of gambling information), section 1341 (relating to mail fraud), section 1343 (relating to wire fraud), section 1344 (relating to financial institution fraud), section 1425 (relating to the procurement of citizenship or nationalization unlawfully), section 1426 (relating to the reproduction of naturalization or citizenship papers), section 1427 (relating to the sale of naturalization or citizenship papers), sections 1461-1465 (relating to obscene matter), section 1503 (relating to obstruction of justice), section 1510 (relating to obstruction of criminal investigations), section 1511 (relating to the obstruction of State or local law enforcement), section 1512 (relating to tampering with a witness, victim, or an informant), section 1513 (relating to retaliating against a witness, victim, or an informant), section 1542 (relating to false statement in application and use of passport), section 1543 (relating to forgery or false use of passport), section 1544 (relating to misuse of passport), section 1546 (relating to fraud and misuse of visas, permits, and other documents), sections 1581-1592 (relating to peonage, slavery, and trafficking in persons), section 1951 (relating to interference with commerce, robbery, or extortion), section 1952 (relating to racketeering), section 1953 (relating to interstate transportation of wagering paraphernalia), section 1954 (relating to unlawful welfare fund payments), section 1955 (relating to the prohibition of illegal gambling businesses), section 1956 (relating to the laundering of monetary instruments), section 1957 (relating to engaging in monetary transactions in property derived from specified unlawful activity), section 1958 (relating to use of interstate commerce facilities in the commission of murder-for-hire), section 1960 (relating to illegal money transmitters), sections 2251, 2251A, 2252, and 2260 (relating to sexual exploitation of children), sections 2312 and 2313 (relating to interstate transportation of stolen motor vehicles), sections 2314 and 2315 (relating to interstate transportation of stolen property), section 2318 (relating to trafficking in counterfeit labels for phonorecords, computer programs or computer program documentation or packaging and copies of motion pictures or other audiovisual works), section 2319 (relating to criminal infringement of a copyright), section 2319A (relating to unauthorized fixation of and trafficking in sound recordings and music videos of live musical performances), section 2320 (relating to trafficking in goods or services bearing counterfeit marks), section 2321 (relating to trafficking in certain motor vehicles or motor vehicle parts), sections 2341-2346 (relating to trafficking in contraband cigarettes), sections 2421-24 (relating to white slave traffic),

(C) any act which is indictable under title 29, United States Code, section 186 (dealing with restrictions on payments and loans to labor organizations) or section 501(c) (relating to embezzlement from union funds),

(D) any offense involving fraud connected with a case under title 11 (except a case under section 157 of this title), fraud in the sale of securities, or the felonious manufacture, importation, receiving, concealment, buying, selling, or otherwise dealing in a controlled substance or listed chemical (as defined in section 102 of the Controlled Substances Act), punishable under any law of the United States,

(E) any act which is indictable under the Currency and Foreign Transactions Reporting Act,

(F) any act which is indictable under the Immigration and Nationality Act, section 274 (relating to bringing in and harboring certain aliens), section 277 (relating to aiding or assisting certain aliens to enter the United States), or section 278 (relating to importation of alien for immoral purpose) if the act indictable under such section of such Act was committed for the purpose of financial gain, or (G) any act that is indictable under any provision listed in section 2332b(g)(5)(B) [federal crimes of terrorism];

(2) "State" means any State of the United States, the District of Columbia, the Commonwealth of Puerto Rico, any territory or possession of the United States, any political subdivision, or any department, agency, or instrumentality thereof;

(3) "person" includes any individual or entity capable of holding a legal or beneficial interest in property;

(4) "enterprise" includes any individual, partnership, corporation, association, or other legal entity, and any union or group of individuals associated in fact although not a legal entity;

(5) "pattern of racketeering activity" requires at least two acts of racketeering activity, one of which occurred after the effective date of this chapter and the last of which occurred within ten years (excluding any period of imprisonment) after the commission of a prior act of racketeering activity;

(6) "unlawful debt" means a debt

(A) incurred or contracted in gambling activity which was in violation of the law of the United States, a State or political subdivision thereof, or which is unenforceable under State or Federal law in whole or in part as to principal or interest because of the laws relating to usury, and

(B) which was incurred in connection with the business of gambling in violation of the law of the United States, a State or political subdivision thereof, or the business of lending money or a thing of value at a rate usurious under State or Federal law, where the usurious rate is at least twice the enforceable rate;

(7) "racketeering investigator" means any attorney or investigator so designated by the Attorney General and charged with the duty of enforcing or carrying into effect this chapter;

(8) "racketeering investigation" means any inquiry conducted by any racketeering investigator for the purpose of ascertaining whether any person has been involved in any violation of this chapter or of any final order,

judgment, or decree of any court of the United States, duly entered in any case or proceeding arising under this chapter;
(9) "documentary material" includes any book, paper, document, record, recording, or other material; and
(10) "Attorney General" includes the Attorney General of the United States, the Deputy Attorney General of the United States, the Associate Attorney General of the United States, any Assistant Attorney General of the United States, or any employee of the Department of Justice or any employee of any department or agency of the United States so designated by the Attorney General to carry out the powers conferred on the Attorney General by this chapter. Any department or agency so designated may use in investigations authorized by this chapter either the investigative provisions of this chapter or the investigative power of such department or agency otherwise conferred by law.

18 U.S.C. 1963. Criminal penalties

(a) Whoever violates any provision of section 1962 of this chapter shall be fined under this title or imprisoned not more than 20 years (or for life if the violation is based on a racketeering activity for which the maximum penalty includes life imprisonment), or both, and shall forfeit to the United States, irrespective of any provision of State law –
(1) any interest the person has acquired or maintained in violation of section 1962;
(2) any –
(A) interest in;
(B) security of;
(C) laim against; or
(D) property or contractual right of any kind affording a source of influence over; any enterprise which the person has established, operated, controlled, conducted, or participated in the conduct of, in violation of section 1962; and
(3) any property constituting, or derived from, any proceeds which the person obtained, directly or indirectly, from racketeering activity or unlawful debt collection in violation of section 1962. The court, in imposing sentence on such person shall order, in addition to any other sentence imposed pursuant to this section, that the person forfeit to the United States all property described in this subsection.

In lieu of a fine otherwise authorized by this section, a defendant who derives profits or other proceeds from an offense may be fined not more than twice the gross profits or other proceeds.

(b) Property subject to criminal forfeiture under this section includes—

(1) real property, including things growing on, affixed to, and found in land; and

(2) tangible and intangible personal property, including rights, privileges, interests, claims, and securities.

(c) All right, title, and interest in property described in subsection (a) vests in the United States upon the commission of the act giving rise to forfeiture under this section. Any such property that is subsequently transferred to a person other than the defendant may be the subject of a special verdict of forfeiture and thereafter shall be ordered forfeited to the United States, unless the transferee establishes in a hearing pursuant to subsection (l) that he is a bona fide purchaser for value of such property who at the time of purchase was reasonably without cause to believe that the property was subject to forfeiture under this section.

(d)(1) Upon application of the United States, the court may enter a restraining order or injunction, require the execution of a satisfactory performance bond, or take any other action to preserve the availability of property described in subsection (a) for forfeiture under this section—

> (A) upon the filing of an indictment or information charging a violation of section 1962 of this chapter and alleging that the property with respect to which the order is sought would, in the event of conviction, be subject to forfeiture under this section; or
>
> (B) prior to the filing of such an indictment or information, if, after notice to persons appearing to have an interest in the property and opportunity for a hearing, the court determines that—
>
> > (i) there is a substantial probability that the United States will prevail on the issue of forfeiture and that failure to enter the order will result in the property being destroyed, removed from the jurisdiction of the court, or otherwise made unavailable for forfeiture; and
> >
> > (ii) the need to preserve the availability of the property through the entry of the requested order outweighs the hardship on any party against whom the order is to be entered:

Provided, however, That an order entered pursuant to subparagraph (B) shall be effective for not more than ninety days, unless extended by the court for good cause shown or unless an indictment or information described in subparagraph (A) has been filed.

(2) A temporary restraining order under this subsection may be entered upon application of the United States without notice or opportunity for a hearing when an information or indictment has not yet been filed with respect to the property, if the United States demonstrates that there is probable cause to believe that the property with respect to which the order is sought would, in the event of conviction, be subject to forfeiture under this section and that provision of notice will jeopardize the availability of the property for forfeiture. Such a temporary order shall expire not more than ten days after the date on which it is entered, unless extended for good cause shown or unless the party against whom it is entered consents to an extension for a longer period. A hearing requested concerning an order entered under this paragraph shall be held at the earliest possible time, and prior to the expiration of the temporary order.

(3) The court may receive and consider, at a hearing held pursuant to this subsection, evidence and information that would be inadmissible under the Federal Rules of Evidence.

(e) Upon conviction of a person under this section, the court shall enter a judgment of forfeiture of the property to the United States and shall also authorize the Attorney General to seize all property ordered forfeited upon such terms and conditions as the court shall deem proper. Following the entry of an order declaring the property forfeited, the court may, upon application of the United States, enter such appropriate restraining orders or injunctions, require the execution of satisfactory performance bonds, appoint receivers, conservators, appraisers, accountants, or trustees, or take any other action to protect the interest of the United States in the property ordered forfeited. Any income accruing to, or derived from, an enterprise or an interest in an enterprise which has been ordered forfeited under this section may be used to offset ordinary and necessary expenses to the enterprise which are required by law, or which are necessary to protect the interests of the United States or third parties.

(f) Following the seizure of property ordered forfeited under this section, the Attorney General shall direct the disposition of the property by sale or any other commercially feasible means, making due provision for the rights of any innocent persons. Any property right or interest not exercisable by, or transferable for value to, the United States shall expire and shall not revert to the defendant, nor shall the defendant or any person acting in concert with or on behalf of the defendant be eligible to purchase forfeited property at any sale held by the United States. Upon application of a person, other than the defendant or a person acting in concert with or on behalf of the defendant, the court may restrain or stay the sale or disposition of the property pending the conclusion of any appeal of the criminal case giving rise to the forfeiture, if the applicant demonstrates that proceeding with the sale or disposition of the property will result in irreparable injury, harm or loss to him. Notwithstanding 31 U.S.C. 3302(b), the proceeds of any sale or other disposition of property forfeited under this section and any moneys forfeited shall be used to pay all proper expenses for the forfeiture and the sale, including expenses of seizure, maintenance and custody of the property pending its disposition, advertising and court costs. The Attorney General shall deposit in the Treasury any amounts of such proceeds or moneys remaining after the payment of such expenses.

(g) With respect to property ordered forfeited under this section, the Attorney General is authorized to—

(1) grant petitions for mitigation or remission of forfeiture, restore forfeited property to victims of a violation of this chapter, or take any other action to protect the rights of innocent persons which is in the interest of justice and which is not inconsistent with the provisions of this chapter;

(2) compromise claims arising under this section;

(3) award compensation to persons providing information resulting in a forfeiture under this section;

(4) direct the disposition by the United States of all property ordered forfeited under this section by public sale or any other commercially feasible means, making due provision for the rights of innocent persons; and

(5) take appropriate measures necessary to safeguard and maintain property ordered forfeited under this section pending its disposition.

(h) The Attorney General may promulgate regulations with respect to—

(1) making reasonable efforts to provide notice to persons who may have an interest in property ordered forfeited under this section;

(2) granting petitions for remission or mitigation of forfeiture;

(3) the restitution of property to victims of an offense petitioning for remission or mitigation of forfeiture under this chapter;

(4) the disposition by the United States of forfeited property by public sale or other commercially feasible means;

(5) the maintenance and safekeeping of any property forfeited under this section pending its disposition; and

(6) the compromise of claims arising under this chapter.

Pending the promulgation of such regulations, all provisions of law relating to the disposition of property, or the proceeds from the sale thereof, or the remission or mitigation of forfeitures for violation of the customs laws, and the compromise of claims and the award of compensation to informers in respect of such forfeitures shall apply to forfeitures incurred, or alleged to have been incurred, under the provisions of this section, insofar as applicable and not inconsistent with the provisions hereof. Such duties as are imposed upon the Customs Service or any person with respect to the disposition of property under the customs law shall be performed under this chapter by the Attorney General.

(i) Except as provided in subsection (l), no party claiming an interest in property subject to forfeiture under this section may–

(1) intervene in a trial or appeal of a criminal case involving the forfeiture of such property under this section; or

(2) commence an action at law or equity against the United States concerning the validity of his alleged interest in the property subsequent to the filing of an indictment or information alleging that the property is subject to forfeiture under this section.

(j) The district courts of the United States shall have jurisdiction to enter orders as provided in this section without regard to the location of any property which may be subject to forfeiture under this section or which has been ordered forfeited under this section.

(k) In order to facilitate the identification or location of property declared forfeited and to facilitate the disposition of petitions for remission or mitigation of forfeiture, after the entry of an order declaring property forfeited to the United States the court may, upon application of the United States, order that the testimony of any witness relating to the property forfeited be taken by deposition and that any designated book, paper, document, record, recording, or other material not privileged be produced at the same time and place, in the same manner as provided for the taking of depositions under Rule 15 of the Federal Rules of Criminal Procedure.

(l)(1) Following the entry of an order of forfeiture under this section, the United States shall publish notice of the order and of its intent to dispose of the property in such manner as the Attorney General may direct. The Government may also, to the extent practicable, provide direct written notice to any person known to have alleged an interest in the property that is the subject of the order of forfeiture as a substitute for published notice as to those persons so notified.

(2) Any person, other than the defendant, asserting a legal interest in property which has been ordered forfeited to the United States pursuant to this section may, within thirty days of the final publication of notice or his receipt of notice under paragraph (1), whichever is earlier, petition the court for a

hearing to adjudicate the validity of his alleged interest in the property. The hearing shall be held before the court alone, without a jury.

(3) The petition shall be signed by the petitioner under penalty of perjury and shall set forth the nature and extent of the petitioner's right, title, or interest in the property, the time and circumstances of the petitioner's acquisition of the right, title, or interest in the property, any additional facts supporting the petitioner's claim, and the relief sought.

(4) The hearing on the petition shall, to the extent practicable and consistent with the interests of justice, be held within thirty days of the filing of the petition. The court may consolidate the hearing on the petition with a hearing on any other petition filed by a person other than the defendant under this subsection.

(5) At the hearing, the petitioner may testify and present evidence and witnesses on his own behalf, and cross-examine witnesses who appear at the hearing. The United States may present evidence and witnesses in rebuttal and in defense of its claim to the property and cross-examine witnesses who appear at the hearing. In addition to testimony and evidence presented at the hearing, the court shall consider the relevant portions of the record of the criminal case which resulted in the order of forfeiture.

(6) If, after the hearing, the court determines that the petitioner has established by a preponderance of the evidence that –

> (A) the petitioner has a legal right, title, or interest in the property, and such right, title, or interest renders the order of forfeiture invalid in whole or in part because the right, title, or interest was vested in the petitioner rather than the defendant or was superior to any right, title, or interest of the defendant at the time of the commission of the acts which gave rise to the forfeiture of the property under this section; or
>
> (B) the petitioner is a bona fide purchaser for value of the right, title, or interest in the property and was at the time of purchase reasonably without cause to believe that the property was subject to forfeiture under this section; the court shall amend the order of forfeiture in accordance with its determination.

(7) Following the court's disposition of all petitions filed under this subsection, or if no such petitions are filed following the expiration of the period provided in paragraph (2) for the filing of such petitions, the United States shall have clear title to property that is the subject of the order of forfeiture and may warrant good title to any subsequent purchaser or transferee.

(m) If any of the property described in subsection (a), as a result of any act or omission of the defendant—

(1) cannot be located upon the exercise of due diligence;
(2) has been transferred or sold to, or deposited with, a third party;
(3) has been placed beyond the jurisdiction of the court;
(4) has been substantially diminished in value; or
(5) has been commingled with other property which cannot be divided without difficulty; the court shall order the forfeiture of any other property of the defendant up to the value of any property described in paragraphs (1) through (5).

18 U.S.C. 1964. Civil remedies

(a) The district courts of the United States shall have jurisdiction to prevent and restrain violations of section 1962 of this chapter by issuing appropriate orders, including, but not limited to: ordering any person to divest himself of any interest, direct or indirect, in any enterprise; imposing reasonable restrictions on the future activities or investments of any person, including, but not limited to, prohibiting any person from engaging in the same type of endeavor as the enterprise engaged in, the activities of which affect interstate or foreign commerce; or ordering dissolution or reorganization of any enterprise, making due provision for the rights of innocent persons.
(b) The Attorney General may institute proceedings under this section. Pending final determination thereof, the court may at any time enter such restraining orders or prohibitions, or take such other actions, including the acceptance of satisfactory performance bonds, as it shall deem proper.
(c) Any person injured in his business or property by reason of a violation of section 1962 of this chapter may sue therefore in any appropriate United States district court and shall recover threefold the damages he sustains and the cost of the suit, including a reasonable attorney's fee, except that no person may rely upon any conduct that would have been actionable as fraud in the purchase or sale of securities to establish a violation of section 1962. The exception contained in the preceding sentence does not apply to an action against any person that is criminally convicted in connection with the fraud, in which case the statute of limitations shall start to run on the date on which the conviction becomes final.
(d) A final judgment or decree rendered in favor of the United States in any criminal proceeding brought by the United States under this chapter shall stop the defendant from denying the essential allegations of the criminal offense in any subsequent civil proceeding brought by the United States.

Bibliography

ALR Fed

Construction and Application of United States Sentencing Guideline §2S1.1 (USSG §2S1/1) Pertaining to Sentencing for Money Laundering, 130 ALR FED 323

Criminalization, Validity, Construction, and Application of 18 USC §1956, Which Criminalizes Money Laundering, 121 ALR FED 525

What Is Considered Property "Involved in" Money Laundering Offense, and Thus Subject to Civil or Criminal Forfeiture, for Purposes of Money Laundering Control Act (18 USCA §981((a)(1)(A) and 982(a)(1)), 135 ALR FED 367

When Does Forfeiture of Currency, Bank Account, Cash Equivalent Violate Excessive Fines Clause of Eight Amendment, 164 ALR FED 591

When Does Forfeiture of Real Property Violate Excessive Fines Clause of Eight Amendment – Post Austin Cases, 168 ALR FED 375

Venue for Currency Reporting Offense Under Currency and Foreign Transactions Report Act (CFTRA)(31 USCA §5311 et seq.), 113 ALR FED 639

Books, Articles, and Notes

Airing the Dirty Laundry: The Application of the United States Sentencing Guidelines to White Collar Money Laundering Offenses, 49 AMERICAN UNIVERSITY LAW REVIEW 289 (1999-2000)

Cassella, The Forfeiture of Property Involved in Money Laundering Offenses, 7 BUFFALO CRIMINAL LAW REVIEW 583 (2004)

The Obstacles to Regulating the Hawala: A Cultural Norm or a Terrorist Hotbed?, 27 FORDHAM INTERNATIONAL LAW JOURNAL 2007 (2004)

Tacking on Money Laundering Charges to White Collar Crimes: What Did Congress Intend, and What Are the Courts Doing, 17 GEORGIA STATE UNIVERSITY LAW REVIEW 531 (2000-2001)

Twenty-Sixth Annual Survey of White Collar Crime: Money Laundering, 48 AMERICAN CRIMINAL LAW REVIEW 929 (2011)

Twenty-Sixth Annual Survey of White Collar Crime: Racketeer Influenced and Corrupt Organizations, 48 AMERICAN CRIMINAL LAW REVIEW 1075 (2011)

United States Money Laundering Threat Assessment Working Group, US MONEY LAUNDERING THREAT ASSESSMENT (December 2005)

Welling, Smurfs, Money Laundering, and the Federal Criminal Law: The Crime of Structuring Transactions, 41 FLORIDA LAW REVIEW 287 (1989)

Williams & Whitney, FEDERAL MONEY LAUNDERING: CRIMES AND FORFEITURE (1999 & 2004 Supp.)

End Notes

[1] Money laundering is "the act of transferring illegally obtained money through legitimate people or accounts so that its original source cannot be traced," BLACK'S LAW DICTIONARY 1097 (9th ed. 2009).

[2] A few years and several amendments ago, one commentator estimated the number of section 1956 predicate offenses at "250 or so," Cassella, *The Forfeiture of Property Involved in Money Laundering Offenses*, 7 BUFFALO CRIMINAL LAW REVIEW 583, 612 (2004). The estimate appears exceptionally conservative. Each of the 50 states outlaws (1) murder, (2) kidnapping, (3) gambling, (4) arson, (5) robbery, (6) bribery, (7) extortion, (8) dealing in obscene material, and (9) drug dealing. A felony violation of any one of these is a section 1956 predicate offense, 18 U.S.C. 1956(c)(7) (A), 1961(1)(A). Each of the close to 200 countries of the world outlaws many if not most of the same types of misconduct (murder, kidnapping, robbery, and the like) and when they do, these too are section 1956 predicate offenses if they involve a financial transaction in the U.S., 18 U.S.C. 1956(c)(7)(B). Yet however daunting the absolute number of section 1956 predicate offenses may be, the reported cases suggest that a handful of predicate offenses (like mail fraud, wire fraud, and drug dealing) account for the vast majority of section 1956 prosecutions.

[3] 18 U.S.C. 1956(a)(1)(B)(ii).

[4] 18 U.S.C. 1956(a)(1)(A)(i).

[5] 18 U.S.C. 1956(a)(2).

[6] 18 U.S.C. 1956(a)(1)(A)(ii).

[7] 18 U.S.C. 1956(a)(1)(B)(ii); 31 U.S.C. 5324.

[8] 18 U.S.C. 1957.

[9] 18 U.S.C. 1952(a)(1).

[10] 18 U.S.C. 1952(a)(3).

[11] 18 U.S.C. 1960(a), (b)(1)(C).

[12] 18 U.S.C. 1960(a), (b)(1)(A), (B).

[13] 31 U.S.C. 5332.

[14] 31 U.S.C. 5322. Federal law features a wide array of administrative, regulatory, and diplomatic anti-money laundering provisions that are beyond the scope of this report.

[15] As a matter of convenience, this report refers to subsections (18 U.S.C. 1956(a)), paragraphs (18 U.S.C. 1956(a)(1)), subparagraphs (18 U.S.C. 1956(a)(1)(A)), clauses (18 U.S.C. 1956(a)(1)(A)(i)), and subclauses as sections.

[16] 18 U.S.C. 1956(a)(1)(A)(i); *United States v. White*, 492 F.3d 380, 397 (6th Cir. 2007); *United States v. Singh*, 518 F.3d 236, 246 (4th Cir. 2008); *United States v. Hudspeth*, 525 F.3d 667, 677 (8th Cir. 2008); *United States v. Brown*, 553 F.3d 768, 782 (5th Cir. 2008); *United States v. Lee*, 558 F.3d 638, 641 (7th Cir. 2009); United States v. Wilkes, 662 F.3d 524, 548 (9th Cir. 2011).

[17] "The term 'knowing that the property involved in a financial transaction represents the proceeds of some form of unlawful activity' means that the person knew the property involved in the transaction represented proceeds from some form, though not necessarily which form, of activity that constitutes a felony under State, Federal, or foreign law, regardless of whether or not such activity is specified in paragraph (7)," 18 U.S.C. 1956(c)(1); *United States v. CedenoPerez*, 579 F.3d 54. 59 (1st Cir. 2009); *United States v Flores*, 454 F.3d 149, 155 (3d Cir. 2006); *United States v. Hill*, 167 F.3d 1055, 1065-68 (6th Cir. 1999).

[18] *United States v. Quinones*, 635 F.3d 590, 594 (2d Cir. 2011)("A conscious avoidance instruction permits a jury to find that a defendant had culpable knowledge of a fact when the evidence shows that the defendant intentionally avoided confirming the fact"); *United States v. Lewis*, 558 F.3d 601, 613 (8th Cir. 2008)("A willful blindness instruction allows the jury to impute knowledge to a defendant of what should be obvious to him, if it found, beyond a reasonable doubt, a conscious purpose to avoid enlightenment"); *United States v. Nektalov*, 461 F.3d 309, 314-15 (2d Cir. 2006); *United States v. Flores*, 454 F.3d 149, 155 (3d Cir. 2006); *cf., United States v. Antzoulatos*, 962 F.2d 720, 725 (7th Cir. 1992) ("It is well settled that wilful blindness or conscious avoidance is the legal equivalent to knowledge....We therefore examine the constitutionality of section 1956(a)(1)(B) as applied to a merchant who actually knew that he was dealing with drug dealers and their money, or deliberately turned a blind eye regarding this fact.... We conclude that Antzoulatos' right to liberty under the Fifth Amendment was not violated").

[19] 18 U.S.C. 1956(c)(2). *United States v. Gotti*, 459 F.3d 296, 335 (2d Cir. 2006)(mere receipt of funds constitutes "conducting a financial transaction"). In spite of the breadth of the definition, an individual must be in control at some point, and in some sense, of the property involved in the transaction, *United States v. Huber*, 404 F.3d 1047, 1060 (8th Cir. 2005)(a defendant does not conduct the financial transfers of third parties which he does not initiate and in he does not participate).

[20] "The term 'transaction' includes a purchase, sale, loan, pledge, gift, transfer, delivery, or other disposition, and with respect to a financial institution includes a deposit, withdrawal, transfer between accounts, exchange of currency, loan, extension of credit, purchase or sale of any stock, bond, certificate of deposit, or other monetary instrument, use of a safe deposit box, or any other payment, transfer, or delivery by, through, or to a financial institution, by whatever means effected," 18 U.S.C. 1956(c)(3); e.g., *United States v. Dvorak*, 617 F.3d 1017, 1023 (8th Cir. 2010); *United States v. Garcia*, 587 F.3d 509, 516 (2d Cir. 2009).

[21] *United States v. Gough*, 152 F.3d 1172, 1173 (9th Cir. 1998); *United States v. Garcia Abrego*, 141 F.3d 142, 160 (5th Cir. 1998); *United States v. Roy*, 375 F.3d 21, 23-4 (1st Cir. 2004)(exchange between individuals of $100 bills for currency of smaller denominations to facilitate drug trafficking); *United States v. Blair*, 661 F.3d 755, 764 (4th Cir. 2011)("Almost any exchange of money between two parties qualifies as a financial transaction subject to

criminal prosecution under §1956, provided that the transaction has at least a minimal effect or on interstate commerce and satisfies at least one of the four intent requirements").

[22] "The term 'financial transaction' means (A) a transaction which in any way or degree affects interstate or foreign commerce (i) involving the movement of funds by wire or other means or (ii) involving one or more monetary instruments, or (iii) involving the transfer of title to any real property, vehicle, vessel, or aircraft, or (B) a transaction involving the use of a financial institution which is engaged in, or the activities of which affect, interstate or foreign commerce in any way or degree," 18 U.S.C. 1956(c)(4).

[23] *United States v. Ables*, 167 F.3d 1021, 1029 (6th Cir. 1999); *United States v. Owens*, 167 F.3d 739, 755 (1st Cir. 1999); *United States v. Bollin*, 264 F.3d 391, 408 (4th Cir. 2001); *United States v. Gotti*, 459 F.3d 296, 336 (2d Cir. 2006); *United States v. Blair*, 661 F.3d 755, 764 (4th Cir. 2011); *e.g., United States v. Hudspeth*, 525 F.3d 667, 680-81 (8th Cir. 2008) (transactions involved checks written on out-of-state banks).

[24] 18 U.S.C. 1956(c)(9).

[25] *United States v. Akintonbi*, 159 F.3d 401, 403 (9th Cir. 1998).

[26] Conducting or attempting to conduct an international transfer to avoid state or federal reporting requirements must involve the proceeds of a crime but the property-generating offense need not be a money laundering predicate, 18 U.S.C. 1956(a)(2)(B)(ii).

[27] 18 U.S.C. 1956(a)(1)(A)(i).

[28] 18 U.S.C. 1956(c)(7)(A).

[29] 18 U.S.C. 1961(1)(A).

[30] "[T]he term 'specified unlawful activity' means ... (B) with respect to a financial transaction occurring in whole or in part in the United States, an offense against a foreign nation involving – (i) the manufacture, importation, sale, or distribution of a controlled substance (as such term is defined for the purposes of the Controlled Substances Act); (ii) murder, kidnapping, robbery, extortion, destruction of property by means of explosive or fire, or a crime of violence (as defined in section 16); (iii) fraud, or any scheme or attempt to defraud, by or against a foreign bank (as defined in paragraph 7 of section 1(b) of the International Banking Act of 1978)); (iv) bribery of a public official, or the misappropriation, theft, or embezzlement of public funds by or for the benefit of a public official; (v) smuggling or export control violations involving – (I) an item controlled on the United States Munitions List established under section 38 of the Arms Export Control Act (22 U.S.C. 2778); or (II) an item controlled under regulations under the Export Administration Regulations (15 C.F.R. Parts 730-774); or (vi) an offense with respect to which the United States would be obligated by a multilateral treaty, either to extradite the alleged offender or to submit the case for prosecution, if the offender were found within the territory of the United States," 18 U.S.C. 1956(c)(7)(B); *United States v. Lazarenko*, 564 F.3d 1026, 1038 (9th Cir. 2009)("The statute clearly lists 'extortion' as a foreign offense that may be a predicate offense for money laundering"); *United States v. One 1997 E35 Ford Van*, 50 F.Supp.2d 789, 797 (N.D.Ill. 1999)("offense against a foreign nation" means an offense in violation of the laws of a foreign nation), *cf.*, *United States v. Magluta*, 418 F.3d 1166, 1173 (11th Cir. 2005).

[31] One Supreme Court Justice referred, tongue-in-cheek, to the RICO predicate offense list as "a laundry list of nearly every federal crime under the sun," *James v. United* States, 550 US 192, 223 (2007)(Scalia, J., dissenting). The more extensive list of federal money laundering predicate offenses appears at the end of this report.

[32] 18 U.S.C. 1956(c)(7)(D)("the term 'specified unlawful activity' means ... an offense under section 351 [offenses against Members of Congress]... 1201 [interstate kidnapping]... 1751 [offenses against the President]...").

[33] 18 U.S.C. 1956(c)(7)(F).
[34] 18 U.S.C. 1956(c)(7)(A).
[35] 18 U.S.C. 1961(1).
[36] *United States v. Santos*, 461 F.3d 886, 889 (7th Cir. 2006).
[37] *Id.* at 891.
[38] 553 U.S. 507, 511 (2008).
[39] Id.
[40] *Id.* at 514.
[41] *Id.* at 515-16.
[42] *Id.* at 524 (Stevens, J. concurring in the judgment).
[43] *Id.* at 525-26 (emphasizing that he could not "agree with the plurality that the rule of lenity must apply to the definition of 'proceeds' for these types of unlawful activities").
[44] *Id.* at 531 (quoting the plurality opinion at 517).
[45] *Id.* n.7. The appended list of federal money predicate offenses notes the maximum term of imprisonment that may be imposed for each of the predicates.
[46] *Id.* at 529 (Alito, J., dissenting).
[47] *Id.* at 538.
[48] *Id.* at 530 (Breyer, J., dissenting)(emphasis in the original)("Thus, like the plurality, I see a 'merger' problem. But, unlike the plurality, I do not believe that we should look to the word 'proceeds' for the solution ... [T]here are other, more legally felicitous places to look for a solution. The Tenth Circuit, for example, has simply held that the money laundering offense and the underlying offense that generated the money to be laundered must be distinct in order to be separately punishable [*United States v. Edgmon,* 952 F.2d 1206, 1214 (10th Cir. 1991)]. Alternatively, the money laundering statute's phrase 'with the intent *to promote* the carrying on of specified unlawful activity' may not apply where, for example, only one instance of that underlying activity is at issue. (The Seventh Circuit on a prior appeal in this case rejected that argument... See *United States v. Febus*, 218 F.3d 784, 789 (2000))").
[49] *United States v. Irvin*, 656 F.3d 1151, 1165 (10th Cir. 2011)("This court has since clarified that *Santos's* holding must be confined to its factual setting, and that 'proceeds' means 'profits' for the purposes of the money laundering statute *only* where an illegal gambling operation is involved"); *United States v. Demarest*, 570 F.3d 1232, 1242 (11th Cir. 2009).
[50] *United States v. Quinones*, 635 F.3d 590, 600 (2d Cir. 2011)("'[P]roceeds' under 18 U.S.C. §1956 is not limited to 'profits' at least where, as here, the predicate offense involves the sale of contraband").
[51] *United States v. Richardson*, 658 F.3d 333, 340 (3d Cir. 2011)("We believe that 'proceeds' means gross receipts in the circumstances of this case. For starters, the merger problem that impelled a majority of the Supreme Court to throw out Santos' conviction is not present here.... Moreover, five justices agreed in *Santos* that 'proceeds' means gross receipts in cases involving the sale of drugs and other contraband.... Finally, out sister circuits uniformly agree that 'proceeds' means receipts in the drug trafficking context – at least where (as here) there is no merger problem"); *United States v. Crosgrove*, 637 F.3d 646, 654-55 (6th Cir. 2011)("'Proceeds' ... means profits only when the §1956 predicate offense creates a merger problem that lead to a radical increase in the statutory maximum sentence and only when nothing in the legislative history suggests that Congress intended such an increase"); *United States v. Rubashkin*, 655 F.3d 849, 866 (8th Cir. 2011)("The narrowest holding in *Santos* was Justice Stevens's concurrence stating that 'proceeds' must mean 'profits whenever a broader definition would 'pervese[ly] result in a 'merger problem.' It follows that the government's argument that proceeds only means profits in the illegal

gambling context can therefore not be correct"); *United States v. Wilkes*, 662 F.3d 524, 549 (9th Cir. 2011)(internal citations omitted)("In *United States v. Van Alstyne*, this court construed *Santos* as a decision 'with less than clear results, but concluded that 'proceeds' means 'profits' where viewing 'proceeds' as 'receipts' would present a 'merger' problem of the kind that troubled the plurality and concurrence in *Santos*. In other words, under *Santos* 'proceeds' as used in 18 U.S.C. §1956 means 'gross receipts' except where the money transfers are 'inherent in the scheme'").

52 18 U.S.C. 1956(c)(9) (emphasis added). Congress added the definition in section 2(f) of P.L. 111-21, 123 Stat. 1618 (2009)(S. 386).

53 *United States v. Yusuf*, 536 F.3d 178, 185 (3d Cir. 2008)(emphasis in the original; some internal citations omitted)("The narrow issue in this appeal is whether unpaid taxes unlawfully disguised and retained by means of the filing of false tax returns through the US mails are 'proceeds' of mail fraud for purposes of sufficiently stating an offense for money laundering....[T]he federal money laundering statute specifically identifies which criminal offenses constitute 'specified unlawful activities. The term 'specified unlawful activities' covers a broad array of offenses. For example, the fraudulent *concealment* of a bankruptcy estate's assets is categorized as a 'specified unlawful activity.' Thus, property which is required to be included in a bankruptcy debtor's estate but is instead undeclared and thus *retained*, is 'proceeds' of a bankruptcy fraud offense....Moreover, simply because funds are *originally* procured through *lawful* activity does not mean that one cannot thereafter convert those same funds into the 'proceeds' of an unlawful activity. *United States v. Levine*, 970 F.2d 681, 686 (10th Cir. 1992)(sustaining money laundering conviction where the defendant concealed corporate tax refund checks deposited in a hidden bank account). Accordingly, we reject the suggestion that to qualify as 'proceeds' under the federal money laundering statute, funds must have been *directly* produced by or through a specified unlawful activity, and we agree that funds *retained* as a result of the unlawful activity can be treated as the 'proceeds' of such crime").

54 *United States v. Yusuf*, 536 F.3d at 186; *United States v. Singh*, 518 F.3d 236, 247 (4th Cir. 2008); *United States v. Szur*, 289 F.3d 200, 213-14 (2d Cir. 2002); *United States v. Richard*, 234 F.3d 763, 770 (1st Cir. 2000).

55 *United States v. Lee*, 558 F.3d 638, 642 (7th Cir. 2009)(payment of the advertising expenses of a prostitution enterprise); *United States v. Lawrence*, 405 F.3d 888, 901 (10th Cir. 2005)(payment of clinic rent in connection with an ongoing Medicare fraud scheme); *United States v. Iacaboni*, 363 F.3d 1, 5, 6 n.9 (1st Cir. 2004)(gambler's pay off of winning bettors, "nothing makes an illegal gambling operation flourish more than the prompt payment of winners," and observing that the "payment of salaries of employees is a common example of promotion within the meaning of the statute"); *United States v. King*, 169 F.3d 1035, 1040 (6th Cir. 1999)(drug dealer's payment for past shipments preserved the defendant's opportunity to acquire additional shipments).

56 *United States v. Brown*, 533 F.3d 768, 786 (5th Cir. 2008)("In examining the question of intent necessary for a money laundering promotion conviction, this court has held that the Government must present either direct proof of an intent to promote such illegal activity, or proof that a given type of transaction on its face, indicates an intent to promote such illegal activity"), quoting, *United States v. Miles*, 360 F.3d 472, 477 (5th Cir. 2004) and *United States v. Brown*, 186 F.3d 661, 670 (5th Cir. 1999).

57 18 U.S.C. 1956(a)(2)(A); *United States v. Caplinger*, 339 F.3d 226, 232 (4th Cir. 2003); *United States v. NarvizGuerra*, 148 F.3d 530, 539 (5th Cir. 1998); *United States v. Anvari-Hamedani*, 378 F.Supp.2d 821, 832 (N.D. Ohio 2005).

[58] "[T]he term 'monetary instruments' means (i) coin or currency of the United States or of any other country, travelers' checks, personal checks, bank checks, and money orders, or (ii) investment securities or negotiable instruments, in bearer form or otherwise in such form that title thereto passes upon delivery," 18 U.S.C. 1956(c)(5).

[59] *United States v. Garcia Abrego*, 141 F.3d 142, 162 n.8 (5th Cir. 1998).

[60] 18 U.S.C. 1956(a)(2)(A); United States v. Moreland, 622 F.3d 1147, 1167 (9th Cir. 2010); *United States v. Krasinski*, 545 F.3d 546, 550-51 (7th Cir. 2008).

[61] *United States v. Trejo*, 610 F.3d 308, 315 (5th Cir. 2010)(" Section 1956(a)(2)(A) contains an identical specific intent requirement for *transportation* cases as its §1956(a)(1)(A)(i) *transaction* counterpart. While the definitive case authority on specific intent derives from the *transaction* provision, it is safe to assume the requirement is no less rigorous under 1956(a)(2)(A). *See United States v. Guezo*, 546 F.3d 174, 179 (2d Cir. 2008) (noting the use of identical language in the transportation and transaction provisions of §1956 is a strong indicator that they should be interpreted in the same manner). We conclude that the same stringent specific intent requirement applies in §1956(a)(2)(A) cases").

[62] *Id.*; *United States v. Caplinger*, 339 F.3d 226, 233 (4th Cir. 2003).

[63] Section 1956(a)(2)(B)(ii)(international transfers to avoid state or federal reporting requirements) has no predicate offense element.

[64] "This amendment to the money laundering statute, 18 U.S.C. 1956, would permit undercover law enforcement officers to pose as drug traffickers in order to obtain evidence necessary to convict money launderers. The present statute does not provide for such operations because it permits a conviction only where the laundered money 'in fact involves the proceeds of specified unlawful activity.'" 134 CONG.REC. 27,420 (1988)(Department of Justice section-bysection analysis inserted by the bill's sponsors).

[65] 18 U.S.C. 1956(a)(3)(A). The terminology used in the section permits an alternative construction of the fourth element. The phrase in question reads "conducts or attempts conduct a financial transaction involving property represented to be the proceeds of specified unlawful activity, or *property used to conduct or facilitate specified unlawful activity*," 18 U.S.C. 1956(a)(3)(emphasis added). It is possible to read the portion in italics as referring to property *represented* to be property used to conduct a predicate offense or alternatively as referring to property that *in fact* constitutes property used to conduct a predicate offense. The first construction seems more consistent with the purpose for adding the section, Williams & Whitney, FEDERAL MONEY LAUNDERING: CRIMES AND FORFEITURE 196-97 (1999 and 2004 Supp.).

[66] 18 U.S.C. 1956(c)(3),(4).

[67] 18 U.S.C. 1956(a)(3).

[68] *United States v. Starke*, 62 F.3d 1374, 1382 (11th Cir. 1995); *United States v. Wydermyer*, 51 F.3d 319, 327-28 (2d Cir. 1995); *United States v. Kaufman*, 985 F.2d 884, 892-93 (7th Cir. 1993).

[69] *United States v. Portalla*, 496 F.3d 23, 28-29 (5th Cir. 2007).

[70] 18 U.S.C. 1956(c)(7).

[71] *Jacobson v. United States*, 503 U.S. 540, 548-49 (1992).

[72] *E.g.*, *United States v. Gurolla*, 333 F.3d 944, 955 (9th Cir. 2003).

[73] Examples of unsuccessful claims appear in *United States v. Ogle*, 328 F.3d 182, 185 (5th Cir. 2003); *United States v. Bala*, 236 F.3d 87, 93-4 (2d Cir. 2000); *United States v. Spriggs*, 102 F.3d 1245, 1260-262 (D.C. Cir. 1996).

[74] 18 U.S.C. 1956(a)(1)(B)(i); *United States v. Wilkes*, 662 F.3d 524, 545 (9th Cir. 2011)("To convict a person of money laundering under 18 U.S.C. §1956(a)(1)(B)(i), the government

must prove that (1) the defendant conducted or attempt to conduct a financial transaction; (2) the transaction involved the proceeds of unlawful activity; (3) the defendant knew that the proceeds were from unlawful activity; and (4) the defendant knew that the transaction was designed in whole or in part ... to conceal or disguise the nature, the location, the source, the ownership, or the control of the proceeds of specified unlawful activity"); *see also United States v. Richardson*, 658 F.3d 333, 337-38 (3d Cir. 2011); *United States v. Heid*, 651 F.3d 850, 855 (8th Cir. 2011); *United States v. Fishman*, 645 F.3d 1175, 1187 (10th Cir. 2011); *United States v. Adefehinti*, 510 F.3d 319, 322 (D.C. Cir. 2008)).

75 18 U.S.C. 1956(c)(1)("[T]he term 'knowing that the property involved in a financial transaction represents the proceeds of some form of unlawful activity' means that the person knew the property involved in the transaction represented the proceeds from some form, though not necessarily which form, of activity that constitutes a felony under State, Federal, or foreign law, regardless of whether or not such activity is specified in paragraph (7)")

76 18 U.S.C. 1956(c)(9).

77 18 U.S.C. 1956(c)(2)

78 E.g., *United States v. Jenkins*, 633 F.3d 788, 804 (9th Cir. 2011).

79 *United States v. Slagg*, 651 F.3d 832, 845 (8th Cir. 2011); *United States v. Naranjo*, 634 F.3d 1198, 1208 (11th Cir. 2011); *United States v. Warshak*, 631 F.3d 266, 323 (6th Cir. 2010); *United States v. Adefehinti*, 510 F.3d 319, 322 (D.C. Cir. 2008); *United States v. Shepard*, 396 F.3d 1116, 1120 (10th Cir. 2005); *United States v. Stephenson*, 183 F.3d 110, 121 (2d Cir. 1999).

80 18 U.S.C. 1956(a)(1)(A)(i), 1956(a)(2)(A).

81 18 U.S.C. 1956(a)(1)(B)(i), 1956(a)(2)(B)(i). The split is not complete. Both sting promotion and the sting concealment prohibitions require no more than an intent to either promote or conceal, 18 U.S.C. 1956(a)(3)(A), (B).

82 *United States v. Heid*, 651 F.3d 850, 855 (8th Cir. 2011).

83 *United States v. Blankenship*, 382 F.3d 1110, 1128-131 (11th Cir. 2004); cf., *United States v. Adefehinti*, 510 F.3d 319, 323-24 (D.C. Cir. 2008).

84 *United States v. Delgado*, 653 F.3d 729, 737 (8th Cir. 2011); see also *United States v. Terkle*, 329 F.3d 1108, 1113- 114 (9th Cir. 2003); cf., *United States v. Dvorak*, 617 F.3d 1017, 1022 (8th Cir. 2010)(emphasis in the original)("The financial transactions identified in the indictment were Dvorak's 'withdrawals of cash from his Wells Fargo Bank account.' The provision of §1956(a)(1)(B)(i) with which we are principally concerned there is whether Dvorak's withdrawals were 'designed in whole or in part to conceal or disguise ... *the location* of the illegal proceeds.... Although cases addressing §1956(a)(1)(B)(i)often focus upon whether the transaction was intended to conceal the 'nature' or 'source' of the funds, a transaction intended to conceal the location of the funds is also a violation of the money laundering statute").

85 *United States v. Magluta*, 418 F.3d 1166, 1176 (11th Cir. 2005); see also *United States v. Baldridge*, 559 F.3d 1126, 1141 (10th Cir. 2009); *United States v. Delgado*, 653 F.3d 729, 738 (8th Cir. 2011)(use or third parties or commingling with legitimate funds); *United States v. Naranjo*, 634 F.3d 1198, (11th Cir. 2011); *United States v. Adefehinti*, 510 F.3d 319, 323 (D.C. Cir. 2008)(listing cases illustrating various deceptive devices).

86 *United States v. Law*, 528 F.3d 888, 896 (D.C.Cir. 2008)("*Cuellar v. United States*, [553 U.S. 550] (2008), held that §1956(a)(2)(B)(i), which prohibits transportation designed to conceal certain attributes of illegally obtained funds, does not require proof that [the] defendant attempted to create [the] appearance of legitimate wealth, but recogniz[ed] [that] such

attempt may signal [a] violation of [the] money laundering statute and indeed is [a] manner in which 'classic money laundering' occurs").

87 18 U.S.C. 1956(a)(2)(B)(i); *United States v. Bieganowski*, 313 F.3d 264, 279 (5th Cir. 2002); *United States v. Ness*, 565 F.3d 73, 77 (2d Cir. 2009); *United States v. Jenkins*, 633 F.3d 788, 806 (9th Cir. 2011).

88 18 U.S.C. 1956(c)(7).

89 18 U.S.C. 1956(a)(2)(B).

90 *Compare, United States v. Kramer*, 73 F.3d 1067, 1072 (11th Cir. 1996)("the jury ... found that Gilbert intended to further the laundering scheme by causing the transfer of $9.5 million from Switzerland to Luxembourg. The jury, however, also found that Gilbert did not cause the transfer of this same money from the United States to Switzerland... the statute does not make money laundering a continuing offense... The jury found that Gilbert was involved in only one transaction and the transaction was totally outside this country. Because this transaction is separate from the one originating in the United States and because money laundering is not a continuing offense, Gilbert's conviction cannot be upheld"); *with, United States v. Harris*, 79 F.3d 223, 231 (2d Cir. 1996)("Harris argues that each time that funds were sent to Switzerland, two transfers took place – one from New York to Connecticut and the other from Connecticut to Switzerland. Harris maintains that it was the transfers of funds from ... New York to ... Connecticut that were designed to conceal the nature ... of the funds ... and not the transfers from Connecticut to Switzerland. Therefore, Harris argues that he should not have been convicted of violating §1956(a)(2). We disagree because we do not interpret the movements of funds from New York to Connecticut and then from Connecticut to Switzerland as two separate events. While the scheme was implemented in two stages, each stage was an integral part of single plan to transfer funds 'from a place in the United States to or through a place outside the United States'"); *United States v. Dinero Express, Inc.*, 313 F.3d 803, 807 (2d Cir. 2002)("a course of conduct that begins with a sum of money located in one country and ends with a related sum of money located in another may constitute a 'transfer' for purposes of §1956(a)(2). This is true whether or not the particular transaction vehicle for effecting the transfer is comprised of a single step or a series, and whether or not the funds move directly between an account in the United States and one abroad").

91 *United States v. Cuellar*, 553 U.S. 550, 563, 566 (2008)(emphasis in the original and some internal citations omitted) ("We agree with petitioner that merely hiding funds during transportation is not sufficient to violate the statute, even if substantial efforts have been expended to conceal the money. Our conclusion turns on the text of §1956(a)(2)(B)(i), and particularly on the term 'design.' In this context, 'design' means purpose or plan; i.e., the intended aim of the transportation....There is a difference between concealing something to transport it and transporting something to conceal it; that is, *how* one moves the money is distinct from *why* one moves the money. Evidence of the former, standing alone, is not sufficient to prove the latter").

92 *Id.*; *United States v. Slagg*, 651 F.3d 832, 845 (8th Cir. 2011)("[T]he Supreme Court held in *Cuellar v. United States* that the statute's 'design' element 'requires proof that the purpose – not merely effect – of the transportation was to conceal or disguise a listed attribute' of the funds.... Thus, the Government must show that concealment is an 'intended aim' of the transaction [or transportation]"); *United States v. Faulkenberry*, 614 F.3d 573, 584-86 (6th Cir. 2010).

[93] *Cuellar v. United States*, 553 U.S. at 557-61 (and noting earlier that several "Courts of Appeals have considered this requirement as relevant or even necessary in the context of 18 U.S.C. 1956(a)(1)(B)(i)," *id.* at 555 n.1).

[94] 18 U.S.C. 1956(a)(2)(B)(emphasis added)).

[95] "[K]nowing that the *property* involved in a financial transaction represent the proceeds of some form of unlawful activity," 18 U.S.C. 1956(a)(1)(emphasis added)).

[96] "[T]he term 'knowing that the property involved in a financial transaction represents the proceeds of some form of unlawful activity' means that the person knew the property involved in the transaction represented proceeds from some form, though not necessarily which form, of activity that constitutes a felony under State, Federal, or foreign law, regardless of whether or not such activity is specified in paragraph (7)," 18 U.S.C. 1956(c)(1).

[97] *United States v. Carr*, 25 F.3d 1194, 1204 (3d Cir. 1994).

[98] 18 U.S.C. 1956(a)(3)(B).

[99] *United States v. Farese*, 248 F.3d 1056, 1060 (11th Cir. 2001).

[100] *United States v. Wolny*, 133 F.3d 758, 760-61 (10th Cir. 1998).

[101] *United States v. Nektalov*, 461 F.3d 309, 314 (2d Cir. 2006).

[102] *Id.* at 314-16.

[103] 18 U.S.C. 1956(c)(4).

[104] *United States v. Oliveros*, 275 F.3d 1299, 1303-304 (11th Cir. 2001).

[105] *United States v. Leslie*, 103 F.3d 1093, 1100 (2d Cir. 1997).

[106] *United States v. Starke*, 62 F.3d 1374, 1382 (11th Cir. 1995); *United States v. Wydermyer*, 51 F.3d 319, 327-28 (2d Cir. 1995); *United States v. Kaufman*, 985 F.2d 884, 892-93 (7th Cir. 1993).

[107] P.L. 91-508, 84 Stat. 1122 (1970), 31 U.S.C. 1051-1122 (1970 ed.).

[108] Welling, *Smurfs, Money Laundering, and the Federal Criminal Law: The Crime of Structuring Transactions*, 41 FLORIDA LAW REVIEW 287, 288 (1989)("[T]he government's opening salvo against laundering [was] a statute requiring financial institutions to report cash transactions over $10,000 to the government. To skirt this law, launderers began to conduct multiple cash transactions just below the $10,000 reporting threshold. The army of persons who scurried from bank to bank to accomplish these transactions became known as 'smurfs' because, like their little blue cartoon namesakes, they were pandemic").

[109] 18 U.S.C. 1956(a)(1)(B)(ii), 1956(a)(2)(B)(ii), and 1956(a)(3)(C), respectively.

[110] 18 U.S.C. 1956(a)(1)(B)(ii); *United States v. Bowman*, 235 F.3d 1113, 1117 (8th Cir. 2000); *United States v. Morales*, 108 F.3d 1213, 1221 (10th Cir. 1997).

[111] *United States v. Bowman*, 235 F.3d at 1118.

[112] *Ratzlaf v. United States*, 510 U.S. 135, 137 (1994).

[113] *United States v. Santos*, 20 F.3d 280, 283 n.2 (7th Cir. 1994).

[114] 18 U.S.C. 1956(c)(1).

[115] 18 U.S.C. 1956(c)(2).

[116] 18 U.S.C. 1956(c)(3),(4).

[117] 18 U.S.C. 1956(c)(7).

[118] 18 U.S.C. 1956(a)(2)(B)(ii); *United States v. Morales*, 108 F.3d 1213, 1221(10th Cir. 1997).

[119] 18 U.S.C. 1956(c)(1); *United States v. Ortiz*, 738 F.Supp. 1394, 1399 (S.D.Fla. 1990) ("This definition [18 U.S.C. 1956(c)(1)] suggests that the statute is applicable to the transportation of the proceeds of any felonious activity where the defendant has knowledge that the proceeds are derived from felonious activity").

[120] 18 U.S.C. 1956(a)(3)(C); *United States v. Nelson*, 66 F.3d 1036, 1040 (9th Cir. 1995)("To prove a violation of this section, the government must prove (1) that the defendant conducted or attempted to conduct a financial transaction, (2) with the intent to avoid a transaction reporting requirement, and (3) that the property involved in the transaction was represented by a law enforcement officer to be the proceeds of specified unlawful activity"); *United States v. Breque*, 964 F.2d 381, 386-87 (5th Cir. 1992).

[121] *United States v. Nelson*, 66 F.3d at 1041 (citing other representation cases to the same effect).

[122] 18 U.S.C. 1956(a)(1)(A)(ii); *United States v. Zanghi*, 189 F.3d 71, 77 (1st Cir. 1999).

[123] *Id.* at 77-8.

[124] "Whoever, conducts or attempts to conduct such a financial transaction ..." 18 U.S.C. 1956(a)(1); "Whoever ... transfers or attempts to ... transfer a monetary instrument ..." 18 U.S.C. 1956(a)(2); "Whoever ... conducts or attempts to conduct a financial transaction involving property represented to be ..." 18 U.S.C. 1956(a)(3).

[125] *United States v. Choy*, 309 F.3d 602, 605 (9th Cir. 2002)(attempt to commit promotional money laundering in violation of section 1956(a)(1)(A)(i)); *United States v. Barnes*, 230 F.3d 311, 314-15 (7th Cir. 2000)(attempt to commit concealment money laundering with an undercover officer in violation of section 1956(a)(3)(B)); *United States v. Nelson*, 66 F.3d 1036, 1042-44 (9th Cir. 1995)(attempt to commit the offense of avoiding reporting requirements with an undercover officer in violation of section 1956(a)(3)(C)).

[126] 18 U.S.C. 371.

[127] "To prove a conspiracy to launder money, the government must demonstrate that the defendant was knowingly involved with two or more people for the purpose of money laundering and that the defendant knew the proceeds used to further the scheme were derived from an illegal activity," *United States v. Turner*, 400 F.3d 491, 496 (7th Cir. 2005); *United States v. Greenidge*, 495 F.3d 85, 100 (4th Cir. 2007).

[128] *Whitfield v. United States*, 543 US 209, 214-18 (2005).

[129] "If two or more persons conspire either to commit any offense against the United States, or to defraud the United States, or any agency thereof in any manner or for any purpose, *and one or more of such persons do any act to effect the object of the conspiracy*, each shall be fined under this title or imprisoned not more than five years, or both...." 18 U.S.C. 371 (emphasis added).

[130] *Whitfield v. United States*, 543 U.S. at 219 (2005); *United States v. Fishman*, 645 F.3d 1175, 1191 (10th Cir. 2011), citing in accord *Whitfield* and *United States v. Green*, 599 F.3d 360, 372 (4th Cir. 2010); *United States v. Prince*, 618 F.3d 551, 553 (6th Cir. 2010).

[131] *United States v. Moreland*, 622 F.3d 1147, 1169 (9th Cir. 2010), citing *Pinkerton v. United States*, 328 US 640, 645-48 (1946).

[132] *United States v. Mowad*, 641 F.2d 1067, 1074-75 (2d Cir. 1981)(conspiracy to attempt to export a firearm illegally in violation of 18 U.S.C. 371 and 22 U.S.C. 2778); *United States v. Clay*, 495 F.2d 700, 710 (7th Cir. 1974)(conspiracy to attempt to burglarize a federally insured bank in violation of 18 U.S.C. 371 and 2113); *United States v. Sierra-Garcia*, 760 F.Supp. 252, 258 (E.D.N.Y. 1991)(conspiracy to attempt money laundering in violation of 18 U.S.C. 371 and 1956).

[133] 18 U.S.C. 2 ("(a) Whoever commits an offense against the United States or aids, abets, counsels, commands, induces or procures its commission, is punishable as a principal. (b) Whoever willfully causes an act to be done which if directly performed by him or another would be an offense against the United States, is punishable as a principal").

[134] *Nye & Nissen v. United States*, 336 U.S. 613, 619 (1949); see also *United States v. Huezo*, 546 F.3d 174, 179-80 (2d Cir. 2008)("To prove that the defendant acted with specific intent, the

government need not establish that he knew all of the details of the crime, only that he joined the venture, that he shared in it, and that his efforts contributed towards its success"); *United States v. Quiles*, 618 F.3d 383, 396 (3d Cir. 2010).

[135] 18 U.S.C. 1956(a).

[136] U.S.S.G. §2S1.1, 52 FED. REG. 44714 (Nov. 20, 1987). The sentencing guidelines were originally considered binding, 18 U.S.C. 3553(b)(1), but now only guide the court's sentencing discretion, *United States v. Booker*, 543 U.S. 220, 258-59 (2005); *Gall v. United States*, 552 U.S. 38, 49 (2007)("[A] district court should begin all sentencing proceedings by correctly calculating the applicable Guidelines range.... [T]he appellate court must review under an abuse-of-discretion standard. It must first ensure that the district court committed no significant procedural error, such as failing to calculate (or improperly calculating) the Guidelines..."). For a discussion of the role the guidelines now play and related policy questions, see CRS Report RL32766, *Federal Sentencing Guidelines: Background, Legal Analysis, and Policy Options*, by Lisa M. Seghetti and Alison M. Smith; for a discussion of the operation of the guidelines, see CRS Report RL32846, *How the Federal Sentencing Guidelines Work: Two Examples*, by Charles Doyle.

[137] United States Sentencing Commission, *Report to the Congress: Sentencing Policy for Money Laundering Offenses, Including Comments on Department of Justice Report* (September 18, 1997), available at http://www.ussc.gov/ Legislative_and_Public_Affairs/Congressional_ Testimony_and_Reports/Money_Laundering_Topics/19970918_RtC_ Money_Laundering.PDF.

[138] U.S.S.G. §2S1.1.

[139] E.g., Mail fraud, once a five-year felony, 18 U.S.C. 1341 (2000 ed.), is now punishable by imprisonment for not more than 20 years, 18 U.S.C. 1341; see also 18 U.S.C. 641 (theft of more than $1000 in federal property, maximum term of imprisonment: 10 years); 201 (bribery of federal officials, maximum term of imprisonment: 15 years). A list of the maximum terms of imprisonment for each of the money laundering predicate offenses appears at the end of this report.

[140] 18 U.S.C. 3583.

[141] 18 U.S.C. 1956(a)(1), (a)(2).

[142] 18 U.S.C. 1956(a)(3), 3571, 3581.

[143] 18 U.S.C. 1956(b)(1).

[144] See generally CRS Report 97-139, *Crime and Forfeiture*, by Charles Doyle.

[145] *E.g.*, 21 U.S.C. 881, 853 (relating to the civil and criminal confiscation of certain property associated with violations of the Controlled Substances Act).

[146] 18 U.S.C. 981(e), 982(b); 21 U.S.C. 881(e), 853(i)(4); 19 U.S.C. 1616a.

[147] "The following property is subject to forfeiture to the United States... (C) Any property, real or personal which constitutes or is derived from proceeds traceable to ... any offense constituting 'specified unlawful activity' (as defined in section 1956(c)(7) of this title), or conspiracy to commit such an offense," 18 U.S.C. 981(a)(1)(C). "If a forfeiture of property is authorized in connection with a violation of an Act of Congress, and any person is charged in an indictment or information with such violation but no specific statutory provision is made for criminal forfeiture upon conviction, the government may include the forfeiture in the indictment or information ... and upon conviction, the court shall order the forfeiture of the property ...." 28 U.S.C. 2461(c).

[148] See e.g., *United States v. Newman*, 659 F.3d 1235, 1239-240 (9th Cir. 2011)("18 U.S.C. §981(a)(1) states: The following property is subject to forfeiture to the United States .... (C) Any property, real or personal, which constitutes or is derived from proceeds traceable to ...

any offense constituting 'specified unlawful activity (as defined in section 1956(c)(7) of this title).... In turn 18 U.S.C. §1956(c)(7) provides that 'the term 'specified unlawful activity' means – (D) an offense under ... section 2113 or 2114 (relating to bank and postal robbery and theft).' Because Newman pleaded guilty to violating 18 U.S.C. §2113, criminal forfeiture is available pursuant to §981(a)(1) (C) and 28 U.S.C. §2461(c)"); *United States v. Gregoire*, 638 F.3d 962, 971 (8th Cir. 2011)("The United States is authorized to seek civil forfeiture of '[a]ny property, real or person, which constitutes or is derived from proceeds traceable to a violation of ' of the offenses specified in 18 U.S.C. §981(a)(1)(C), which include mail fraud and interstate transportation of stolen property. See 18 U.S.C. §§1956(a)(7)(A)").

[149] "The following property is subject to forfeiture to the United States: (A) Any property, real or personal, involved in a transaction or attempted transaction in violation of section 1956... of this title or any property traceable to such property which constitutes or is derived from proceeds traceable to ... any offense," 18 U.S.C. 981(a)(1)(A). "The court, in imposing sentence on a person convicted of an offense in violation of section 1956 ... of this title, shall order that the person forfeit to the United States any property, real or personal involved in such offense, or any property traceable to such property," 18 U.S.C. 982(a)(1).

[150] *United States v. Seher*, 562 F.3d 1344, 1368 (11th Cir. 2009)(internal quotation marks and citations omitted).

[151] *United States v. Huber*, 404 F.3d 1047, 1058 (8th Cir. 2005); *United States v. Baker*, 227 F.3d 955, 970 (7th Cir. 2000); *United States v. Tencer*, 107 F.3d 1120, 1134 (5th Cir. 1997). The term also includes "any commissions or fees paid to the launderer, and any property used to facilitate the laundering offense," *United States v. Bornfield*, 145 F.3d 1123, 1135 (10th Cir. 1998).

[152] Cassella, *The Forfeiture of Property Involved in Money Laundering Offenses*, 7 BUFFALO CRIMINAL LAW REVIEW 583, 627 (2004)(the "government may get a money judgment for the amount involved in the conversion of [tainted] proceeds to consumer goods, or it may forfeit the converted property itself, but it cannot forfeit both"), citing *United States v. Hawley*, 148 F.3d 920, 928 (8th Cir. 1998).

[153] *United States v. Bajakajian*, 524 U.S. 321, 334 (1998).

[154] *Bajakajian* found an attempted forfeiture, based on anti-money laundering reporting statute, excessive, *Id.*

[155] E.g., *United States v. Wyly*, 193 F.3d 289, 303 (5th Cir. 1999); *United States v. Bollin*, 264 F.3d 391, 417-19 (4th Cir. 2001); *United States v. Misla-Aldarondo*, 478 F.3d 52, 72 (1st Cir. 2007); *United States v. Seher*, 562 F.3d 1344, 1371 (11th Cir. 2009)("A forfeiture order violates the Excessive Fines Clause if it 'is grossly disproportional to the gravity of a defendant's offense.' To make this determination, we principally look at three factors: (1) whether the defendant falls into the class of persons at whom the criminal statute was principally directed; (2) other penalties authorized by the legislature (or the Sentencing Commission); and (3) the harm caused by the defendant"), quoting *United States v. Bajakajian*, 524 U.S. 321, 327 (1998).

[156] U.S.Const. Art.III, §2, cl.3; Amend. VI.

[157] United States v. Cabrales, 524 U.S.1 (1998).

[158] United States v. Cabrales, 524 U.S. at 3-4.

[159] 18 U S.C. 1956(i)("(1) Except as provided in paragraph (2), a prosecution for an offense under this section or section 1957 may be brought in – (A) any district in which the financial or monetary transaction is conducted; or (B) any district where a prosecution for the underlying specified unlawful activity could be brought, if the defendant participated in the

transfer of the proceeds of the specified unlawful activity from that district to the district where the financial or monetary transaction is conducted. (2) A prosecution for an attempt or conspiracy offense under this section or section 1957 may be brought in the district where venue would lie for the completed offense under paragraph (1), or in any other district where an act in furtherance of the attempt or conspiracy took place").

160 Section "1957 is often called the 'money spending statute.' Its purpose is to make the criminal's money worthless, by making it a felony for him to spend it, or for anyone else to take it, if he knows of its illegal source," Cassella, *The Forfeiture of Property Involved in Money Laundering Offenses*, 7 BUFFALO CRIMINAL LAW REVIEW 583, 614 (2004).

161 *United States v. Rutgard*, 116 F.3d 1270, 1291 (9th Cir. 1997)("The description of the crime [under section 1957] does not speak to the attempt to cleanse dirty money by putting it in a clean form and so disguising it. This statute applies to the most open, above-board transaction"); *United States v. Gabriele*, 63 F.3d 61, 65(1st Cir. 1995)("The crux of the argument is that section 1957 is a rather novel statute, in that it criminalizes conduct by a person once removed from that of the person who generated the criminally derived property. Thus, he argues, the proscribed conduct is not likely to appear unlawful to an ordinary citizen... Section 1957 is but another in a substantial line of federal criminal statutes whose only *mens rea* requirement is knowledge of the prior criminal conduct that tainted the property involved in the proscribed activity").

162 "(a) Whoever, in any of the circumstances set forth in subsection (d), knowingly engages or attempts to engage in a monetary transaction in criminally derived property that is of a value greater than $10,000 and is derived from specified unlawful activity, shall be punished as provided in subsection (b). "(d) The circumstances referred to in subsection (a) are – (1) that the offense under this section takes place in the United States or in the special maritime and territorial jurisdiction of the United States; or (2) that the offense under this section takes place outside the United States and such special jurisdiction, but the defendant is a United States person (as defined in section 3077 of this title, but excluding the class described in paragraph (2)(D) of such section). "(f) As used in this section– (1) the term 'monetary transaction' means the deposit, withdrawal, transfer, or exchange, in or affecting interstate or foreign commerce, of funds or a monetary instrument (as defined in section 1956(c)(5) of this title) by, through, or to a financial institution (as defined in section 1956 of this title), including any transaction that would be a financial transaction under section 1956(c)(4)(B) of this title, but such term does not include any transaction necessary to preserve a person's right to representation as guaranteed by the sixth amendment to the Constitution; (2) the term 'criminally derived property' means any property constituting, or derived from, proceeds obtained from a criminal offense; and (3) the term 'specified unlawful activity' has the meaning given that term in section 1956 of this title," 18 U.S.C. 1957(a), (d), (f).

163 *United States v. Irvin*, 656 F.3d 1151, 1165-166 (10th Cir. 2011); see also *United States v. Wetherald*, 636 F.3d 1315, 1325 n.2 (11th Cir. 2011); *United States v. Shafer*, 608 F.3d 1056, 1067 (8th Cir. 2010); *United States v. Greenidge*, 497 F.3d 85, 100 (3d Cir. 2007).

164 "(4) [T]he term 'financial transaction' means (A) a transaction which in any way or degree affects interstate or foreign commerce (i) involving the movement of funds by wire or other means or (ii) involving one or more monetary instruments, or (iii) involving the transfer of title to any real property, vehicle, vessel, or aircraft, or (B) a transaction involving the use of a financial institution which is engaged in, or the activities of which affect, interstate or foreign commerce in any way or degree," 18 U.S.C. 1956(c)(4). "(3) [T]he term 'transaction' includes a purchase, sale, loan, pledge, gift, transfer, delivery, or other

disposition, and with respect to a financial institution includes a deposit, withdrawal, transfer between accounts, exchange of currency, loan, extension of credit, purchase or sale of any stock, bond, certificate of deposit, or other monetary instrument, use of a safe deposit box, or any other payment, transfer, or delivery by, through, or to a financial institution, by whatever means effected," 18 U.S.C. 1956(c)(3).

165 "(f) As used in this section – (1) the term 'monetary transaction' means the deposit, withdrawal, transfer, or exchange, in or affecting interstate or foreign commerce, of funds or a monetary instrument (as defined in section 1956(c)(5) of this title) by, through, or to a financial institution (as defined in section 1956 of this title), including any transaction that would be a financial transaction under section 1956(c)(4)(B) of this title, but such term does not include any transaction necessary to preserve a person's right to representation as guaranteed by the sixth amendment to the Constitution," 18 U.S.C. 1957(f)(1).

166 *United States v. Wright*, 651 F.3d 764, 771-72 (7th Cir. 2011).

167 "[T]he term 'financial institution' includes – (A) any financial institution, as defined in section 5312(a)(2) of title 31, United States Code, or the regulations promulgated thereunder; and (B) any foreign bank, as defined in section 1 of the International Banking Act of 1978 (12 U.S.C. 3101)," 18 U.S.C. 1956(c)(6). "'[F]inancial institution' means – (A) an insured bank (as defined in section 3(h) of the Federal Deposit Insurance Act (12 U.S.C. 1813(h))); (B) a commercial bank or trust company; (C) a private banker; (D) an agency or branch of a foreign bank in the United States; (E) any credit union; (F) a thrift institution; (G) a broker or dealer registered with the Securities and Exchange Commission under the Securities Exchange Act of 1934 (15 U.S.C. 78a et seq.); (H) a broker or dealer in securities or commodities; (I) an investment banker or investment company; (J) a currency exchange; (K) an issuer, redeemer, or cashier of travelers' checks, checks, money orders, or similar instruments; (L) an operator of a credit card system; (M) an insurance company; (N) a dealer in precious metals, stones, or jewels; (O) a pawnbroker; (P) a loan or finance company; (Q) a travel agency; (R) a licensed sender of money or any other person who engages as a business in the transmission of funds, including any person who engages as a business in an informal money transfer system or any network of people who engage as a business in facilitating the transfer of money domestically or internationally outside of the conventional financial institutions system; (S) a telegraph company; (T) a business engaged in vehicle sales, including automobile, airplane, and boat sales; (U) persons involved in real estate closings and settlements; (V) the United States Postal Service; (W) an agency of the United States Government or of a State or local government carrying out a duty or power of a business described in this paragraph; (X) a casino, gambling casino, or gaming establishment with an annual gaming revenue of more than $1,000,000 which – (i) is licensed as a casino, gambling casino, or gaming establishment under the laws of any State or any political subdivision of any State; or (ii) is an Indian gaming operation conducted under or pursuant to the Indian Gaming Regulatory Act other than an operation which is limited to class I gaming (as defined in section 4(6) of such Act); (Y) any business or agency which engages in any activity which the Secretary of the Treasury determines, by regulation, to be an activity which is similar to, related to, or a substitute for any activity in which any business described in this paragraph is authorized to engage; or (Z) any other business designated by the Secretary whose cash transactions have a high degree of usefulness in criminal, tax, or regulatory matters," 31 U.S.C. 5312(a)(2).

168 *United States v. Benjamine*, 252 F.3d 1, 9 (1st Cir. 2001)("Section 1957(f) only requires that the transactions have a de minimis effect on commerce"); *United States v. Ables*, 167 F.3d

1021, 1030-31 (6th Cir. 1999); *United States v. Aramony*, 88 F.3d 1369, 1386 (4th Cir. 1995).

169 18 U.S.C. 1957(a); *United States v. Irvin*, 656 F.3d 1151, 1164 (10th Cir. 2011); *United States v. Gamory*, 635 F.3d 480, 496 (11th Cir. 2011); *United States v. Gallardo*, 497 F.3d 727, 737 (7th Cir. 2007).

170 "In a prosecution for an offense under this section, the Government is not required to prove the defendant knew that the offense from which the criminally derived property was derived was specified unlawful activity," 18 U.S.C. 1957(c); *United States v. Flores*, 454 F.3d 149, 155 (3d Cir. 2006); *United States v. Carucci*, 364 F.3d 339, 343 (1st Cir. 2004); *United States v. Foreman*, 323 F.3d 498, 506 (6th Cir. 2003). Nor need the defendant be charged with or convicted of the predicate offense, *United States v. Cherry*, 330 F.3d 658, 667 (4th Cir. 2003); *United States v. Richard*, 234 F.3d 763, 768 (1st Cir. 2000). Moreover, "[k]nowledge may be demonstrated by showing that the defendant either had actual knowledge or deliberately closed his eyes to what otherwise would have been obvious to him concerning the fact in question," *United States v. Flores*, 454 F.3d at 155.

171 18 U.S.C. 1957(a); *United States v. Diamond*, 378 F.3d 720, 728 (7th Cir. 2004)("In order to find Diamond guilty of this offense [under section 1957], the government needed to prove that she derived property from a specified unlawful activity and that she engaged in a monetary transaction").

172 18 U.S.C. 1957(f)(3); 18 U.S.C. 1956(c)(9)("[T]he term 'proceeds' means any property derived from or obtained or retained, directly or indirectly, thorough some form of unlawful activity, including the gross receipts of such activity").

173 18 U.S.C. 1957(f)(1).

174 *United States v. Blair*, 661 F.3d 755, 771 (4th Cir. 2011)("[T]he scope of the safe harbor provision is shaped by the Sixth Amendment. Thus, anyone seeking to befit from §1957(f) must tie his conduct to the Sixth Amendment right to counsel"); *United States v. Velez*, 586 F.3d 875, 877 (11th Cir. 2009)("Accordingly, the exemption is limited to attorneys' fees paid for representation guaranteed by the Sixth Amendment in a criminal proceeding and does not extend to attorneys' fees paid for other purposes"); *United States v. Hoogenboom*, 209 F.3d 665, 669 (7th Cir. 2000)("Correctly read, the statute offers a defense where a defendant engages in a transaction underlying a money laundering charge with the present intent of exercising Sixth Amendment rights. This allows a defendant to preserve her rights without undermining the prosecution of those the statute seeks to punish. Since Hoogenboom did not clear her accounts to pay her attorney – the evidence is that she engaged in the transaction to prevent the FBI from seizing the money – she cannot squeeze within the slim Sixth Amendment exception to the statute's broad definition of what constitutes a monetary transaction").

175 *United States v. Elso*, 422 F.3d 1305, 1309 (11th Cir. 2005).

176 18 U.S.C. 1957(a)("Whoever ... engages or attempts to engage ...").

177 *E.g., United States v. Resendez-Ponce*, 549 U.S. 102, 107 (2007); see also, *United States v. Pires*, 642 F.3d 1, 9 (1st Cir. 2011); *United States v. Manzo*, 636 F.3d 56, 66 (3d Cir. 2011); *United Stats v. Farhane*, 634 F.3d 127, 145 (2d Cir. 2011); *United States v. Sanchez*, 615 F.3d 836, 843 (7th Cir. 2010); *United States v. Robertson*, 606 F.3d 943, 953 (8th Cir. 2010).

178 *E.g., United States v. Choy*, 309 F.3d 602, 605 (9th Cir. 2002); *United States v. Barnes*, 230 F.3d 311, 314 (7th Cir. 2000).

179 *United States v. Wittig*, 575 F3d 1085, 1103 (10th Cir. 2009).

180 *Whitfield v. United States*, 543 U.S. 209, 211 (2005).

181 *United States v. Silvestri*, 409 F.3d 1311, 1335-336 (11th Cir. 2005).

[182] 18 U.S.C. 2; *United States v. Dadi*, 235 F.3d 945, 951 (5th Cir. 2000)(internal citations and quotation marks omitted)("Dadi also disputes the sufficiency of the evidence to support the aiding and abetting charges. To convict under 18 U.S.C. 1957, the government must prove that the defendant knowingly engaged or attempted to engage in a monetary transaction in criminally derived property that is of a value greater than $10,000 and is derived from specified unlawful activity. To prove that a defendant aided and abetted the commission of a criminal offense, the government must show that the defendant intentionally associated with, and participated in, the criminal venture and acted to make the venture succeed").

[183] Offenders convicted of an offense carrying a maximum penalty of 25 years or more are ineligible for probation by statute, 18 U.S.C. 3561(a)(1), 3581(b). Under the guidelines, even a first time offender whose offense level is more than 10 is ineligible for probation and a first time offender whose offense level is 9 or 10 is only eligible as part of a split sentence, U.S.S.G. §5B1.1, Sentencing Table. The money laundering sentencing guideline calls for a base offense level equal to that of the predicate offense if ascertainable or otherwise a base offense level of 8; the base offense level is increased by 1 level for a violation of section 1957 and another 2 levels if offense involved sophisticated laundering, U.S.S.G. §2S1.1. Most five-year felonies carry a base offense level of 8 or more, e.g., U.S.S.G. §2b5.3 (base offense level of 8) (criminal copyright infringement), §2H3.1 (base offense level of 9) (wiretapping). Many section 1956 predicate offenses carry a maximum penalty of at least five years, e.g., 18 U.S.C. 1343 (wire fraud: 20 years), 641 (theft of more than $1000 in federal property: 10 years); 201 (bribery of federal officials: 15 years).

[184] 18 U.S.C. 3561(c)(1).

[185] 18 U.S.C. 3583.

[186] 18 U.S.C. 1957(b), 1956(h), 3571, 3559.

[187] 18 U.S.C. 1956(b)(1).

[188] 18 U.S.C. 981(a)(1)(A),982(a)(1)(A).

[189] The Act in its entirety reads: "(a) Whoever travels in interstate or foreign commerce or uses the mail or any facility in interstate or foreign commerce, with intent to – (1) distribute the proceeds of any unlawful activity; or (2) commit any crime of violence to further any unlawful activity; or (3) otherwise promote, manage, establish, carry on, or facilitate the promotion, management, establishment, or carrying on, of any unlawful activity, and thereafter performs or attempts to perform– (A) an act described in paragraph (1) or (3) shall be fined under this title, imprisoned not more than five years, or both; or (B) an act described in paragraph (2) shall be fined under this title, imprisoned for not more than 20 years, or both, and if death results shall be imprisoned for any term of years or for life. (b) As used in this section (i) "unlawful activity" means (1) any business enterprise involving gambling, liquor on which the Federal excise tax has not been paid, narcotics or controlled substances (as defined in section 102(6) of the Controlled Substances Act), or prostitution offenses in violation of the laws of the State in which they are committed or of the United States, (2) extortion, bribery, or arson in violation of the laws of the State in which committed or of the United States, or (3) any act which is indictable under subchapter II of chapter 53 of title 31, United States Code, or under section 1956 or 1957 of this title and (ii) the term "State" includes a State of the United States, the District of Columbia, and any commonwealth, territory, or possession of the United States. (c) Investigations of violations under this section involving liquor shall be conducted under the supervision of the Attorney General," 18 U.S.C. 1952.

[190] *United States v. Hinojosa*, 958 F.2d 624, 629 (5th Cir. 1992).

191 *United States v. Driver*, 535 F.3d 424, 430 (6th Cir. 2008); *United States v. Nishnianidze*, 342 F.3d 6, 15 (1st Cir. 2003); *United States v. Welch*, 327 F.3d 1081, 1090 (10th Cir. 2003); *United States v. Burns*, 298 F.3d 523, 537 (6th Cir. 2002); *United States v. Xiong*, 262 F.3d 672, 676 (7th Cir. 2001); *United States v. James*, 210 F.3d 1342, 1345 (11th Cir. 2000); *United States v. Bankston*, 182 F.3d 296, 315 (5th Cir. 1999).

192 *United States v. Salameh*, 152 F.3d 88, 152 (2d Cir. 1998); see also *United States v. Dinwiddie*, 618 F.3d 821, 832 (8th Cir. 2010)(The government was required to prove: (1) Dinwiddie and Meador traveled, or caused and aided and abetted another to travel in interstate commerce: (2) Dinwiddie and Meador did so with the intent to commit a crime of violence in the furtherance of unlawful activity; (3) Dinwiddie and Meador knowingly and willfully committed a crime of violence; or caused and aided and abetted another to do so, in furtherance of the unlawful activity; and (4) [in capital case] the death of Burgos resulted").

193 *United States v. Corona*, 885 F.2d 766, 773 (11th Cir. 1989).

194 *United States v. Lightfoot*, 506 F.2d 238, 242 (D.C. Cir. 1974); *United States v. Cole*, 704 F.2d 554, 558 (11th Cir. 1983).

195 *United States v. Lignarolo*, 770 F.2d 971, 980 (11th Cir. 1985).

196 *United States v. Corona*, 885 F.2d at 774 ("Ray Corona helped Fernandez buy controlling interest in a bank under extremely dishonest circumstances with laundered drug money. Such a purchase is in reality part of the laundering process. For his role in the purchase and in running the bank for Fernandez, Ray received a percentage ownership without paying any of the purchase price. In essence, Fernandez bought the bank with drug proceeds and gave a portion of it to Ray.... Although Ray Corona was the recipient, he nonetheless was responsible under 18 U.S.C. 2 as principal in the distribution of the proceeds").

197 *United States v. Welch*, 327 F.3d 1081, 1091 (10th Cir. 2003); *United States v. Jones*, 909 F.2d 533, 539 (D.C. Cir. 1990).

198 *United States v. Burns*, 298 F.3d 523, 538 (6th Cir. 2002)("By associating with Green in Kentucky and by remaining in the car that Green intended to use to leave the scene of the drug sale at the Newport bar [following their trip from Ohio], Jordon placed himself in the position to (1) receive immediate payment from Green after the sale in Kentucky, (2) provide surveillance support, and (3) physically aid Green should any danger arise. Thus, Jordon acted, while in Kentucky, in furtherance of the intended unlawful act there"); *United States v. Harris*, 903 F.2d 770, 773 (10th Cir. 1990)("the illegal activity charged was possession of marijuana with intent to distribute. Defendant traveled into Oklahoma from Maryland, Virginia, and Tennessee. He performed various overt acts in furtherance of the crime charged after arriving in Oklahoma, including possessing and transporting a quantity of marijuana with the intent to distribute it").

199 *United States v. Welch*, 327 F.3d 1081, 1092 (10th Cir. 2003) ("an individual may violate the Travel Act simply by attempting to perform a specified 'unlawful act' so long as that individual has the requisite intent"); *United States v. Burns*, 298 F.3d 523, 537-38 (6th Cir. 2002)(internal citations and quotation marks omitted)("the *Zolicoffer* court made clear that its holding should not be interpreted to say that the government must prove that the defendant committed an illegal act after the travel, but only that a plain reading of the statute shows that it must prove some conduct after the travel in furtherance of the unlawful activity").

200 *United States v. Nader*, 542 F.3d 713, 717-22 (9th Cir. 2008)(Travel Act reaches intrastate use of the telephone); see also *United States v. Nishnianidze*, 342 F.3d 6, 15 (1st Cir. 2003); *United States v. Baker*, 227 F.3d 955, 962 (7th Cir. 2000); *United States v. Jenkins*, 943 F.2d

167, 172 (2d Cir. 1991); *United States v. Graham*, 856 F.2d 756, 760-61 & n.1 (6th Cir. 1988).

[201] *United States v. Baker*, 82 F.3d 273, 275 (8th Cir. 1996).

[202] *United States v. Rogers*, 387 F.3d 925, 935 (7th Cir. 2004); *United States v. Auerbach*, 913 F.2d 407, 410 (7th Cir. 1990).

[203] Of course, interstate travel and interstate shipment will do as well, *United States v. Xiong*, 262 F.3d 672, 676 (7th Cir. 2001); *cf.*, *Erlenbaugh v. United States*, 409 U.S. 239, 240-42 (1972).

[204] United States v. Baker, 82 F.3d at 275; United States v. Auerbach, 913 F.2d at 410.

[205] *United States v. Baker*, 82 F.3d at 275-76; *United States v. McNeal*, 77 F.3d 938, 944 (7th Cir. 1996); *United States v. Houlihan*, 92 F.3d 1271, 1292 (1st Cir. 1996).

[206] 18 U.S.C. 1952(b)(3)("any act which is indictable under subchapter II of chapter 53 of title 31, United States Code, or under section 1956 or 1957 of this title"); *United States v. Jenkins*, 943 F.2d 167, 173 (2d Cir. 1991); *United States v. Al-Arian*, 308 F.Supp.2d 1322, 1353 (M.D.Fla. 2004).

[207] *United States v. Nardello*, 393 U.S. 286, 294-96 (1969); *Perrin v. United States*, 444 U.S. 37, 49 (1979); *Scheidler v. NOW*, 537 U.S. 393, 409-10 (2003).

[208] 18 U.S.C. 1952(b)(1); *United States v. Dailey*, 24 F.3d 1323, 1328 (11th Cir. 1994) ("Congress chose to attack organized crime through selectively defining the term 'unlawful activity.' Congress made certain offenses in areas typically associated with organized crime, i.e., gambling, liquor, narcotics, and prostitution, 'unlawful activities' only if engaged in by a 'business enterprise'").

[209] *United States v. Roberson* 6 F.3d 1088, 1094 (5th Cir. 1993); see also *United States v. James*, 210 F.3d 1342, 1345 (11th Cir. 2000); *United States v. Saget*, 991 F.2d 702, 712 (11th Cir. 1993)("If the defendant engages in a continuous course of cocaine distribution rather than a sporadic or casual course of conduct, then the statutory requirement of a business enterprise involving narcotics is satisfied"); *United States v. Iennaco*, 893 F.2d 394, 398 (D.C. Cir. 1990).

[210] *United States v. Griffin*, 85 F.3d 284, 287-88 (7th Cir. 1996); *United States v. Campione*, 942 F.2d 429, 433-36 (7th Cir. 1991); *United States v. Jones*, 909 F.2d 533, 536-39 (D.C.Cir. 1990).

[211] *United States v. Childress*, 58 F.3d 693, 721 (D.C.Cir. 1995)(citing the *Pinkerton* principle of coconspirator liability); see also *United States v. Auerbach*, 913 F.2d 407, 410 (7th Cir. 1990) (co-conspirator liability); *United States v. Dinwiddie*, 618 F.3d 821, 832 (8th Cir. 2010); *United States v. Rogers*, 387 F.3d 925, 935 (7th Cir. 2004)("To meet its burden on the alleged violations of 18 U.S.C. 2 and 1952, the government had to show that Mr. Owens knowingly aided and abetted another person's interstate travel with the intent of promoting the [drug trafficking] offense"); *United States v. Lee*, 359 F.3d 194, 209 (3d Cir. 2004)(aiding and abetting); *United States v. Stott*, 245 F.3d 890, 909 (7th Cir. 2001)(aiding and abetting); *United States v. Pardue*, 983 F.2d 943, 945-46 (8th Cir. 1993)(aiding and abetting); *United States v. Dischner*, 974 F.2d 1502, 1521 (9th Cir. 1992)(aiding and abetting).

[212] 18 U.S.C. 1952(a)(A).

[213] 18 U.S.C. 1952(a)(B).

[214] 18 U.S.C. 3571, 3559.

[215] 18 U.S.C. 3583.

[216] 18 U.S.C. 1952, 981, 982.

[217] 21 U.S.C. 853, 881.

[218] 18 U.S.C. 1961(1)(B), 1956(c)(7)(A), 1957(f)(3).

[219] 18 U.S.C. 981((a)(1)(A), 982(a)(1); see e.g., *United States v. Reiner*, 500 F.3d 10, 13, 18-9 (1st Cir. 2007)(upholding a forfeiture incurred as a consequence of conviction for "interstate travel to promote prostitution, 18 U.S.C. 1952 (the Travel Act); inducement to instate travel to engage in prostitution, 18 U.S.C. 2422(a)(the Mann Act); conspiracy to violate the Travel Act and the Mann Act, 18 U.S.C. 371; and conspiracy to launder money, 18 U.S.C. 1956(h) and 1957"); *United States v. Saccoccia*, 433 F.3d 19, 23 (1st Cir. 2005)(noting confiscation as a consequence of a conviction of "one count of RICO conspiracy, as well as numerous substantive ... counts of money laundering and related offenses under 18 U.S.C. 1952, 1956, and 1957").

[220] The text of 31 U.S.C. 5322 appears at the end of this report.

[221] 31 U.S.C. 5322(a).

[222] 31 U.S.C. 5322(b), (d).

[223] *Ratzlaf v. United States*, 510 U.S. 135, 137 (1994); *United States v. Tatoyan*, 474 F.3d 1174, 1177 (9th Cir. 2007).

[224] 18 U.S.C. 1952(b)(3), 1961(1)(E).

[225] 18 U.S.C. 1956(c)(7)(A), 1957(f)(3).

[226] 31 U.S.C. 5317(c).

[227] *United States v. Bajakajian*, 524 U.S. 321, 324 (1998).

[228] 524 U.S. 321, 324 (1998).

[229] *United States v. $100,348.00*, 354 F.3d 1110, 1123-124 (9th Cir. 2003)(affirming the confiscation of $10,000 of the $100,348 originally seized); *United States v. Beras*, 183 F.3d 22, 28 (1st Cir. 1999)(overturning as an excessive fine the forfeiture order for $138,794 in unreported cash); *United States v. One Hundred and Twenty Thousand Eight Hundred and Fifty Six Dollars*, 394 F.Supp.2d 687, 692-96 (D.V.I. 2005)(holding that confiscation of more than $7500 of the unreported $120,856 would constitute an excessive fine); *United States v. $293,316*, 349 F.Supp.2d 638, 650 (E.D.N.Y. 2004)(ordering the confiscation of $48,000 of the $490,000 of unreported cash seized).

[230] *United States v. $293,316*, 349 F.Supp.2d at 648-49 (listing 168 instances where unreported cash was forfeited and noting that in a vast majority of cases, at least 90% of the cash was confiscated).

[231] 18 U.S.C. 1956(a)(1)(B)(ii), (a)(2)(B)(ii), (a)(3)(C), discussed *supra*, outlaw certain financial transactions and international monetary transfers designed to avoid state or federal reporting requirements.

[232] Both sections were enacted as part of Subtitle I-H (the Money Laundering Control Act of 1986) of the Anti-Drug Abuse Act of 1986, 100 Stat. 3207-18, 3207-22 (1986).

[233] 31 U.S.C. 5322, 5313 (1982 ed.).

[234] *United States v. Winfield*, 997 F.2d 1076, 1082-83 (4th Cir. 1993); *United States v. Nersesian*, 824 F.2d 1294, 1313 (2d Cir. 1987). The federal conspiracy statute outlaws two types of conspiracy – conspiracy to violate another federal criminal law and conspiracy to defraud the United States. Conspiracy to defraud the United States is the agreement to take some action, which might otherwise be lawful, that interferes with or obstructs some governmental function by trickery or deceit, *Hammerschmidt v. United States*, 265 U.S. 182, 188 (1924).

[235] 31 U.S.C. 5324 (1988 ed.). The criminal penalties for willful violation of section 5324 were then found in section 5322, 18 U.S.C. 5322 (1988 ed.).

[236] "No person shall, for the purpose of evading the reporting requirements of section 5313(a)[cash transactions involving $10,000 or more] or 5325 [issuing cashiers' checks of

$3,000 or more] or any regulation prescribed under any such section, the reporting or recordkeeping requirements imposed by any order issued under section 5326 [geographic anti-money laundering requirements], or the recordkeeping requirements imposed by any regulation prescribed under section 21 of the Federal Deposit Insurance Act [12 U.S.C. 1829b (record keeping by federally insured depository institutions)]or section 123 of Public Law 91-508 [12 U.S.C. 1953 (record keeping by uninsured institutions)] – (1) cause or attempt to cause a domestic financial institution to fail to file a report required under section 5313(a) or 5325 or any regulation prescribed under any such section, to file a report or to maintain a record required by an order issued under section 5326, or to maintain a record required pursuant to any regulation prescribed under section 21 of the Federal Deposit Insurance Act or section 123 of Public Law 91-508; (2) cause or attempt to cause a domestic financial institution to file a report required under section 5313(a) or 5325 or any regulation prescribed under any such section, to file a report or to maintain a record required by any order issued under section 5326, or to maintain a record required pursuant to any regulation prescribed under section 5326, or to maintain a record required pursuant to any regulation prescribed under section 21 of the Federal Deposit Insurance Act or section 123 of Public Law 91-508, that contains a material omission or misstatement of fact; or (3) structure or assist in structuring, or attempt to structure or assist in structuring, any transaction with one or more domestic financial institutions," 31 U.S.C. 5324(a).

[237] "(b) No person shall, for the purpose of evading the report requirements of section 5331 [cash transactions involving $10,000 or more] or any regulation prescribed under such section – (1) cause or attempt to cause a nonfinancial trade or business to fail to file a report required under section 5331 or any regulation prescribed under such section; (2) cause or attempt to cause a nonfinancial trade or business to file a report required under section 5331 or any regulation prescribed under such section that contains a material omission or misstatement of fact; or (3) structure or assist in structuring, or attempt to structure or assist in structuring, any transaction with 1 or more nonfinancial trades or businesses," 31 U.S.C. 5324(b).

[238] "No person shall, for the purpose of evading the reporting requirements of section 5316 [importing or exporting $10,000 or more in cash] – (1) fail to file a report required by section 5316, or cause or attempt to cause a person to fail to file such a report; (2) file or cause or attempt to cause a person to file a report required under section 5316 that contains a material omission or misstatement of fact; or (3) structure or assist in structuring, or attempt to structure or assist in structuring, any importation or exportation of monetary instruments," 31 U.S.C. 5324(c).

[239] 31 U.S.C. 5324(a)-(c).

[240] *United States v. Sweeney*, 611 F.3d 459, 471-73(8th Cir. 2009); *United States v. Van Allen*, 524 F.3d 814, 820-21 (7th Cir. 2008).

[241] 31 U.S.C. 5324(d).

[242] 31 U.S.C. 5317(c)(2); *United States v. $79,650.00 (Afework)*, 650 F.3d 381, 383 n.3 (4th Cir. 2011).

[243] *United States v. Chaplin's, Inc.*, 646 F.3d 846, 851-55(11th Cir. 2011)(forfeiture order in the amount of almost $1.9 million was not excessive considering, among other factors, that the Sentencing Guidelines would permit a fine of $1.3 million).

[244] Section 5322 now reads, "(a) A person willfully violating this subchapter or a regulation prescribed or order issued under this subchapter (except section 5315 or 5324 of this title or a regulation prescribed under section 5315 or 5324), or willfully violating a regulation prescribed under section 21 of the Federal Deposit Insurance Act or section 123 of Public Law 91-508, shall be fined not more than $250,000, or imprisoned for not more than five

years, or both. (b) A person willfully violating this subchapter or a regulation prescribed or order issued under this subchapter (except section 5315 or 5324 of this title or a regulation prescribed under section 5315 or 5324), or willfully violating a regulation prescribed under section 21 of the Federal Deposit Insurance Act or section 123 of Public Law 91-508, while violating another law of the United States or as part of a pattern of any illegal activity involving more than $100,000 in a 12-month period, shall be fined not more than $500,000, imprisoned for not more than 10 years, or both. (c) For a violation of section 5318(a)(2) of this title or a regulation prescribed under section 5318(a)(2), a separate violation occurs for each day the violation continues and at each office, branch, or place of business at which a violation occurs or continues. (d) A financial institution or agency that violates any provision of subsection (i) or (j) of section 5318, or any special measures imposed under section 5318A, or any regulation prescribed under subsection (i) or (j) of section 5318 or section 5318A, shall be fined in an amount equal to not less than 2 times the amount of the transaction, but not more than $1,000,000."

[245] P.L. 103-325, 108 Stat. 2253 (1994), 31 U.S.C. 5324(c)(2000 ed.), now 31 U.S.C. 5324(d).

[246] *Ratzlaf v. United States*, 510 U.S. 135, 137 (1994).

[247] *United States v. Sweeney*, 611 F.3d 459, 470 (8th Cir. 2010)(The crime of currency structuring ... has three elements, which are: One, the defendant conducted or attempted to conduct a financial transaction; Two, at the time the defendant conducted or attempted to conduct the financial transaction, the defendant knew of the domestic financial institution's obligation to report currency transactions in excess of $10,000; and Three, the defendant purposefully structured the transaction with the intent to evade that reporting requirement"); *United States v. Van Allen*, 524 F.3d 814, 820 (7th Cir. 2008); *United States v. MacPherson*, 424 F.3d 183, 189 (2d Cir. 2005); *United States v. Bringier*, 405 F.3d 310, 314-15 (5th Cir. 2005); *United States v. Boyd*, 180 F.3d 967, 981 (8th Cir. 1999)(supplying a casino with false identification with the knowledge that the misinformation would be included in the casino's currency transaction report constitutes a material misstatement in violation of section 5324(a)(2)).

[248] 524 U.S. 321, 324 (1998).

[249] "Whoever, with the intent to evade a currency reporting requirement under section 5316, knowingly conceals more than $10,000 in currency or other monetary instruments on the person of such individual or in any conveyance, article of luggage, merchandise, or other container, and transports or transfers or attempts to transport or transfer such currency or monetary instruments from a place within the United States to a place outside of the United States, or from a place outside the United States to a place within the United States, shall be guilty of a currency smuggling offense and subject to punishment pursuant to subsection (b)," 31 U.S.C. 5332(a).

[250] *E.g., United States v. Ely*, 468 F.3d 399, 400 (6th Cir. 2006); *United States v. Peleti*, 576 F.3d 377, 380 (7th Cir. 2009).

[251] *United States v. Tatoyan*, 474 F.3d 1174, 1179-179 (9th Cir. 2007).

[252] "For purposes of this section, the concealment of currency on the person of any individual includes concealment in any article of clothing worn by the individual or in any luggage, backpack, or other container worn or carried by such individual," 31 U.S.C. 5332(b). In fact, the Money Laundering Threat Assessment Working Group report noted in 2005 that the largest bulk cash smuggling seizures, both in terms of numbers of seizures and amount seized, involve cash that was "unconcealed," *U.S. Money Laundering Threat Assessment*, 39 (561 seizures ($243 million) of unconcealed cash versus the next highest category (515

seizures ($83.8) from luggage)), available at http://www.ustreas.gov/offices/ enforcement /pdf/mlta.pdf.

[253] "In addition, the court, in imposing sentence under paragraph (1), shall order that the defendant forfeit to the United States, any property, real or personal, involved in the offense, and any property traceable to such property. The seizure, restraint, and forfeiture of property under this section shall be governed by section 413 of the Controlled Substances Act. If the property subject to forfeiture under paragraph (2) is unavailable, and the defendant has insufficient substitute property that may be forfeited pursuant to section 413(p) of the Controlled Substances Act, the court shall enter a personal money judgment against the defendant for the amount that would be subject to forfeiture," 31 U.S.C. 5332(b)(2)(caption omitted.). "Any property involved in a violation of subsection (a), or a conspiracy to commit such violation, and any property traceable to such violation or conspiracy, may be seized and forfeited to the United States. The seizure and forfeiture shall be governed by the procedures governing civil forfeitures in money laundering cases pursuant to section 981(a)(1)(A) of title 18, United States Code. For purposes of this subsection and subsection (b), any currency or other monetary instrument that is concealed or intended to be concealed in violation of subsection (a) or a conspiracy to commit such violation, any article, container, or conveyance used, or intended to be used, to conceal or transport the currency or other monetary instrument, and any other property used, or intended to be used, to facilitate the offense, shall be considered property involved in the offense," 31 U.S.C. 5332(c)(caption omitted).

[254] H.Rept. 107-250, at 37 (2001)("[I]n response to the *Bajakajian* decision, the Department of Justice proposed making the act of bulk cash smuggling itself a criminal offense, and to authorize the imposition of the full range of civil and criminal sanctions when the offense is discovered. Because the act of concealing currency for the purpose of smuggling it out of the United States is inherently more serious than simply failing to file a Customs report, strong and meaningful sanctions, such as confiscation of the smuggled currency, are likely to withstand Eighth Amendment challenges to the new statute"); see also *United States v. $293,316*, 349 F.Supp.2d 638, 643 (E.D.N.Y. 2004); Cassella, *Bulk Cash Smuggling and the Globalization of Crime: Overcoming Constitutional Challenges to Forfeiture Under 31 U.S.C. 5332*, 22 BERKELEY JOURNAL OF INTERNATIONAL LAW 98, 106 (2004)("In 2001, Congress expressed its displeasure with the *Bajakajian* decision and created a new 'bulk cash smuggling' offense, 31 U.S.C. 5332, that is designed to permit forfeiture of one hundred percent of the smuggled currency in most circumstances, whether or not the government can establish a nexus between the smuggled money and another criminal offense. Enacted as part of the post-September 11 effort to address terrorist financing specifically, and intentional money laundering generally, in Title II of the USA PATRIOT Act, the new law recognizes the central role that bulk cash smuggling plays in the globalization of crime").

[255] *United States v. Ely*, 468 F.3d 399, 402 n.2 (6th Cir. 2006)("This statute included a forfeiture provision that was a precursor of the present version of 31 U.S.C. 5332. The statutory language was modified as part of the USA PATRIOT Act in 2001, by moving the forfeiture provisions from 18 U.S.C. 982 (the statute authorizing the forfeiture in *Bajakajian*") to 31 U.S.C. 5332 (the statute authorizing Ely's forfeiture). The government advances this modification as a basis for us to find *Bajakajian* inapplicable. However, the forfeiture language of the two provisions is virtually identical, and even if Congress could circumvent the Eighth Amendment's limitations on excessive fines by modifying a statute, which would make little sense, cutting and pasting a provision of the United States Code from one

chapter to another cannot be viewed as a meaningful change"); but see *United States v. Jose*, 499 F.3d 105, 110-11(1st Cir. 2007) ("Congress, in enacting section 5332, responded to *Bajakajian* in a way that it believed would, in most circumstances, constitutionally permit the full forfeiture of currency not reported to authorities as required by section 5316 ... Section 5332 makes clear that Congress has now prohibited what it calls 'bulk cash smuggling,' and that it considers this to be a very serious offense. Congress has thus tipped the forfeiture equation in favor of the prosecution in bulk cash smuggling cases. *Bajakajian* itself stated that 'judgments about the appropriate punishment for an offense belong in the first instance to the legislature'").

256 18 U.S.C. 1960(a)("Whoever knowingly conducts, controls, manages, supervises, directs, or owns all or part of an unlicensed money transmitting business shall be fined in accordance with this title and imprisoned for not more than 5 years, or both").

257 "'[M]oney transmitting' includes transferring funds on behalf of the public by any and all means including but not limited to transfers within this country or to locations abroad by wire, check, draft, facsimile, or courier," 18 U.S.C. 1960(b)(2).

258 *United States v. Banki*, 660 F.3d 665, 679 (2d Cir. 2011)(internal quotation marks and citations omitted)("[T]o find a defendant liable for operating an unlicensed money transmitting business, a jury must find that he participated in more than a single, isolated transmission of money. Likewise, given the term 'business' its plain and unambiguous meaning under §1960 a business is an enterprise that is carried on for profit or financial gain").

259 18 U.S.C. 1960(b)(1).

260 18 U.S.C. 1960(b)(1)(A)("'[U]nlicensed money transmitting business' means a money transmitting business which affects interstate or foreign commerce in any manner or degree and – (A) is operated without an appropriate money transmitting license in a State where such operation is punishable as a misdemeanor or a felony under State law, whether or not the defendant knew that the operation was required to be licensed or that the operation was so punishable").

261 *United States v. Elfgeeh*, 515 F.3d 100, 133 (2d Cir. 2008); *United States v. Talebnejad*, 460 F.3d 563, 568 (4th Cir. 2006); *United States v. Mazza-Alaluf*, 607 F.Supp.2d 484, 489 (S.D.N.Y. 2009), aff'd, 621 F.3d 205 (2d Cir. 2010)(conviction requires proof beyond a reasonable doubt that "1.) Mazza knowingly conducted, controlled, managed, supervised, directed, or owned 2.) a money-transmitting business that 3.) affected interstate or foreign commerce, and 4.) was not in compliance with applicable licensing requirements under either state or federal law").

262 18 U.S.C. 1960(b)(1)(A)(quoted above).

263 18 U.S.C. 1960(b)(1)(B)("'[U]nlicensed money transmitting business' means a money transmitting business which affects interstate or foreign commerce in any manner or degree and ... (B) fails to comply with the money transmitting business registration requirements under section 5330 of title 31, United States Code, or regulations prescribed under such section").

264 *United States v. Talebnejad*, 460 F.3d 563, 568 (4th Cir. 2006).

265 *United States v. Uddin*, 365 F.Supp.2d 825, 828-30 (E.D.Mich. 2005).

266 "'[U]nlicensed money transmitting business' means a money transmitting business which affects interstate or foreign commerce in any manner or degree and ... (C) otherwise involves the transportation or transmission of funds that are known to the defendant to have been derived from a criminal offense or are intended to be used to promote or support unlawful activity," 18 U.S.C. 1960(b)(1)(C).

[267] 18 U.S.C. 1960(a), 3571, 3553.

[268] 18 U.S.C. 981(a)(1)(A), 982(a)(1); see *e.g.*, *United States v. $715,031.27*, 587 F.Supp.2d 1275, 1277-278 (N.D.Ga. 2008); cf., *United States v. e-Gold, Ltd*, 521 F.3d 411, 412-13 (D.C.Cir. 2008).

[269] *United States v. Dimitrov*, 546 F.3d 406, 414-15 (7th Cir. 2008); *United States v. Talenejad*, 460 F.3d at 568.

[270] 18 U.S.C. 1956(c)(7)(A), 1957(f)(3).

[271] Mail fraud and wire fraud, 18 U.S.C. 1341, 1343, are RICO predicates, 18 U.S.C. 1961(1)(B), but are not individually listed as money laundering predicates under sections 1956 and 1957, 1956(c)(7)(B). Nevertheless, as RICO predicates, they are by definition money laundering predicates and permit prosecution under sections 1956 and 1957, see *e.g.*, *United States v. Lazarenko*, 564 F.3d 1026, 1032 (9th Cir. 2009); *United States v. Freeman*, 434 F.3d 369, 374 (5th Cir. 2005); *United States v. Yousuf*, 536 F.3d 178, 182 (9th Cir. 2008); *United States v. Boscarino*, 437 F.3d 634, 636 (7th Cir. 2006) ("Section 1956 makes it a crime to engage in financial transactions with the proceeds of 'specified unlawful activity.' That phrase, a defined term, includes 'any act or activity constituting an offense listed in section 1961(1) of this title'").

[272] *E.g.*, *United States v. Fiander*, 547 F.3d 1036, 1037 (9th Cir. 2008); *United States v. DeLaMata*, 535 F.3d 1267, 1269 (11th Cir. 2008); *United States v. Ghilarducci*, 480 F.3d 542, 545 (7th Cir. 2007); *United States v. Gotti*, 459 F.3d 296, 301 (2d Cir. 2006); *United States v. Edwards*, 303 F.3d 606, 612 (5th Cir. 2002).

[273] E.g., *United States v. Rosse*, 320 F.3d 170, 173 (2d Cir. 2003); *United States v. Farese*, 248 F.3d 1056, 1058 (11th Cir. 2001).

[274] 18 U.S.C. 1962(c). Other subsections of 18 U.S.C. 1962 outlaw acquiring, or maintaining control of, a commercial enterprise through collection of an unlawful debt or a pattern of racketeering and proscribe conspiracy to commit a RICO offense, 18 U.S.C. 1962(a), (b), (d).

[275] *United States v. Brandao*, 539 F.3d 44, 50-1 (1st Cir. 2008); see also *United States v. Knight*, 659 F.3d 1285, 1288 (10th Cir. 2011); *United States v. Bergrin*, 650 F.3d 257, 265 (3d Cir. 2011); *United States v. Fowler*, 535 F.3d 408, 418 (6th Cir. 2008).

[276] *United States v. Tocco*, 200 F.3d 401, 426 (6th Cir. 2000)(indictment based on the collection of illegal gambling proceeds). Although the "collection of unlawful debts" may clearly include loan sharking (18 U.S.C. 891-896 (relating to extortionate credit transactions)), the collection of an unlawful debt need not involve the violence or the threat of violence required of extortionate credit transactions. The concept of "collection of an unlawful debt" embodies usury and the collection of gambling debts with or without violence, 18 U.S.C. 1961(6); *e.g.*, *Cannarozzi v. Fiumara*, 371 F.3d 1, 3-4 (1st Cir. 2004); *Neild v. Wolpoff & Abramson, L.L.P.*, 453 F.Supp.2d 918, 926 (E.D.Va. 2006).

[277] 18 U.S.C. 1961(3).

[278] 18 U.S.C. 1961(4).

[279] United States v. Bergrin, 650 F.3d 257, 266 (3d Cir. 2011); City of New York v. Smokes-Spirits.Com, Inc., 541 F.3d 425, 446-47 (2d Cir. 2008); Abraham v. Singh, 480 F.3d 351, 357 (5th Cir. 2007); Living Designs, Inc. v. E.I.Dupont de Nemours and Co., 431 F.3d 353, 361 (9th Cir. 2005); Branon v. Boatmen's First National Bank, 153 F.3d 1144, 1146 (10th Cir. 1998); United States v. London, 66 F.3d 1227, 1244 (1st Cir. 1995); Cedric Kushner Promotions, Ltd. v. King, 533 U.S. 158, 161 (2001)(holding, however, that the "person" and the individual through whom a corporate enterprise acts may be the same and need not be distinct).

[280] *Boyle v. United States*, 129 S.Ct. 2337, 2346 (2009); see also, *United States v. Bingham*, 653 F.3d 983, 992 (9th Cir. 2011); *United States v. Bergrin*, 650 F.3d 257, 265-66 (3d Cir. 2011); *United States v. Applins*, 637 F.3d 59, 73 (2d Cir. 2011).

[281] *United States v. Robertson*, 514 U.S. 669, 671 (1995); proof of even a de minimis effect on interstate commerce is sufficient where the enterprise is engaged in economic activity, *United States v. Nascimento*, 491 F.3d 25, 37-45 (1st Cir. 2007); *United States v. Gardiner*, 463 F.d 445, 458 (6th Cir. 2006); *United States v. Smith*, 413 F.3d 1253, 1274- 275 (10th Cir. 2005); *United States v. Rodriguez*, 360 F.3d 949, 955 (9th Cir. 2004); *United States v. Gray*, 137 F.3d 765, 773 (4th Cir. 1998).

[282] 18 U.S.C. 1961(5); *United States v. Burden*, 600 F.3d 204, 216 (2d Cir. 2010); *Clark v. Time Warner Cable*, 523 F.3d 1110, 1116 (9th Cir. 2008).

[283] "A pattern is not formed by sporadic activity.... [A] person cannot be subjected to the sanctions [of RICO] simply for committing two widely separate and isolated criminal offenses. Instead, the term 'pattern' itself requires the showing of a relationship between the predicates and of the threat of continuing activity. It is this factor of *continuity plus relationship* which combines to produce a pattern," *H.J., Inc. v. Northwestern Bell Telephone Co.*, 492 U.S. 229, 239 (1989)(emphasis of the Court); *United States v. Cianci*, 378 F.3d 71, 88 (1st Cir. 2004); *United States v. Delgado*, 401 F.3d 290, 298 (5th Cir. 2005); *United States v. Burden*, 600 F.3d 204, 216 (2d Cir. 2010); *United States v. Bradley*, 644 F.3d 1213, 1238 (11th Cir. 2011); *United States v. Knight*, 659 F.3d 1285, 1288-289 (10th Cir. 2011). Prior conviction of a predicate offense, however, is not required or even usual, *BancOklahoma Mortgage Corp. v. Capital Title Co.*, 194 F.3d 1089, 1102 (10th Cir. 1999); *cf., Sedima, S.P.R.L. v. Imrex Co., Inc.*, 473 U.S. 479, 488-93 (1985)(a private cause of action under RICO does not require the prior conviction of a defendant).

[284] *H.J., Inc. v. Northwestern Bell Telephone Co.,* 492 U.S. at 240, quoting 18 U.S.C. 3575(e); see also *United States v. Knight*, 659 F.3d 1285, 1289-292 (10th Cir. 2011); *United States v. Bingham*, 653 F.3d 983, 992 (9th Cir. 2011); *United States v. Eppolito*, 543 F.3d 25, 51 (2d Cir. 2008); *United States v. Brandao*, 539 F.3d 44, 55 (1st Cir. 2008); *United States v. Browne*, 505 F.3d 1229, 1257-258 (11th Cir. 2007).

[285] *H.J.,Inc. v. Northwestern Bell Tel.Co.*, 492 U.S. at 241("'continuity' is both a closed- and open-ended concept, referring either to a closed end period of repeated conduct, or to past conduct that by its nature projects into the future with a threat of repetition"); *United States v. Bergin*, 650 F.3d 257, 267 (3dCir. 2011); *United States v. Bradley*, 644 F.3d 1213, 1238 (11th Cir. 2011); *United States v. Wilson*, 605 F.3d 985, 1021-22 (D.C.Cir. 2010).

[286] *Spool v. World Child International Adoption Agency*, 520 F.3d at 184 ("we have never held a period of less than two years to constitute a substantial period of time" sufficient to constitute a closed ended RICO pattern); *Primary Care Investors, Seven v. PHP Healthcare Corp.*, 986 F.2d 1208, 1215 (8th Cir. 1993)(holding predicate offenses over 10-11 months insufficient and citing cases finding several years sufficient but several periods of less than a year insufficient); *United States v. Browne*, 505 F.3d at 1263 (holding predicate offenses over a five-year period sufficient to show a closed ended RICO pattern).

[287] *United States v. Torres*, 191 F.3d 799, 808 (7th Cir. 1999)("As other courts of appeals have noted, in cases where the acts of the defendant or the enterprise were inherently unlawful, such as murder or obstruction of justice, and where in pursuit of inherently unlawful goals, such as narcotics trafficking or embezzlement, the courts generally have concluded that the requisite threat of continuity was adequately established by the nature of the activity, even though the period spanned by the racketeering activity was short"); *Spool v. World Child International Adoption Agency*, 520 F.3d at 184. Open ended continuity may also be found

where the evidence suggests that only the intervention of law enforcement authorities closed down the enterprise, *United States v. Richardson*, 167 F.3d 621, 626-27 (D.C.Cir. 1999); *Jackson v. BellSouth Telecommunications*, 372 F.3d 1250, 1267 (11th Cir. 2004); *United States v. Connolly*, 341 F.3d 16, 30 (1st Cir. 2003).

[288] *United States v. Yannotti*, 541 F.3d 112, 121-22 (2d Cir. 2008); *United States v. Browne*, 505 F.3d at 1263-264; *United States v. Olson*, 450 F.3d 655, 664 (7th Cir. 2006).

[289] *Salinas v. United States*, 522 U.S. 52, 63 (1997); *United States v. Smith*, 413 F.3d 1253, 1265 (10th Cir. 2005); *United States v. Browne*, 505 F.3d at 1263-264.

[290] 18 U.S.C. 1963(a).

[291] 18 U.S.C. 1963(a), (b).

[292] 18 U.S.C. 1964(c).

[293] 18 U.S.C. 1964(a). The question of whether injunctions and other forms of equitable relief are available to private plaintiffs or only to the government has thus far divided the lower federal courts, *Religious Tech. Center v. Wollersheim*, 796 F.2d 1076, 1082-86 (9th Cir. 1986)(private plaintiffs are not entitled to equitable relief under RICO); *Minter v. Wells Fargo Bank,* 593 F.Supp.2d 788, 795-96 (D.Md. 2009)(same); *American Medical Association v. United Healthcare Corp.*, 588 F.Supp.2d 432, 444-46 (S.D.N.Y. 2008)(same); *contra, National Organization for Women, Inc. v. Scheidler*, 267 F.3d 687, 695-700 (7th Cir. 2001)(private RICO plaintiffs are eligible for equitable relief), *rev'd on other grounds,* 537 U.S. 393 (2003); *In re Managed Care Litigation*, 298 F.Supp.2d 1259, 1281-283 (S.D. Fla. 2003)(same); *Chambers Development Co., Inc. v. Browning-Ferris Industries*, 590 F.Supp. 1528, 1540-541 (W.D.Pa. 1984)(same); see also *Scheidler v. National Organization for Women, Inc.*, 537 U.S. at 411 (finding it unnecessary to resolve the issue in the case before it).

[294] However, "[m]any courts have applied the logic of *Central Bank* [*v. First Interstate Bank,* 511 U.S. 164(1994)] to RICO and concluded that §1962(c) does not provide for [civil] aiding and abetting liability, *Cobbs v. Sheahan*, 385 F.Supp.2d 731, 738 (N.D.Ill. 2005); *accord, DeFalco v. Bernas,* 244 F.3d 286, 330 (2d Cir. 2001)*; Pennsylvania Association of Edwards Heirs v. Rightenour*, 235 F.3d 839, 840 (3d Cir. 2000*)*; *In re Countrywide Financial Corp. Mortgage Marketing and Sales Practice*, 601 F.Supp.2d 1201, 1219 (S.D.Cal. 2009); *Rolo v. City Investing Co. Liquidating Trust*, 155 F.3d 644, 656-68 (3d Cir. 1998); *In re MasterCard International Inc., Internet Gambling Litigation*, 132 F.Supp.2d 468, 493-95 (E.D.La. 2001), *aff'd*, 313 F.3d 257 (5th Cir. 2002); *contra, In re Managed Care Litigation*, 298 F.Supp.2d at 1272; see also *First American Corp. v. Al-Nahyan,* 17 F.Supp.2d 10, 23-4 (D.D.C. 1998)(preliminarily finding *Central Bank* distinguishable, but finding it unnecessary to resolve the issue in light of the prospect of the defendants' possible direct RICO liability); *American Automotive Accessories, Inc. v. Fishman*, 991 F.Supp. 987, 993 (N.D.Ill. 1998)("to be held liable as an aider and abettor, a person must in some sort associate himself with the venture, participate in it as something he wishes to bring about, and seek by his action to make it succeed")(noting that the Seventh Circuit has yet to "comment on the possibility of aiding and abetting liability in civil RICO actions").

[295] * RICO predicate offense.

[296] Here and in several other instances, the death penalty is an alternative sanction when commission of the offense results in a death.

[297] **A federal crime of terrorism that as such constitutes a RICO predicate and therefore a money laundering predicate and that is not otherwise listed on either RICO or money laundering predicate lists; crimes which are both money laundering predicates and federal crimes of terrorism or RICO offenses *e.g.*, 18 U.S.C. 32 (destruction of aircraft) are not identified with **.

[298] ~ "Act or activity constituting an offense involving a federal health care offense" not otherwise listed as a money laundering predicate offense, 18 U.S.C. 1956(c)(7)(F).

In: Money Laundering
Editors: C. Bennett and C. Turner
ISBN 978-1-62081-614-1

Chapter 2

UNITED STATES V. SANTOS: "PROCEEDS" IN FEDERAL CRIMINAL MONEY LAUNDERING STATUTE, 18 U.S.C. SECTION 1956, MEANS "PROFITS," NOT "GROSS RECEIPTS"*

M. Maureen Murphy

SUMMARY

On June 2, 2008, the U. S. Supreme Court, in *United States v. Santos* (No. 06-1005), vacated convictions of the operator of an illegal lottery and one of his runners who had been charged with conducting financial transactions involving the "proceeds" of an illegal gaming business in violation of 18 U.S.C. § 1956. The ruling is that "proceeds," as used in this money laundering statute, means "profits" rather than "gross receipts" of the underlying unlawful activity. The decision combines a plurality opinion interpreting the word "proceeds" in the statute to mean "profits" and a concurring opinion, necessary for a majority ruling, that leaves room for interpreting "proceeds" as "gross receipts" in other circumstances. A strong dissenting opinion emphasized the constraints the ruling will place on prosecutors. The interpretation rests on two principles of statutory construction: the rule of lenity and the merger

* This is an edited, reformatted and augmented version of Congressional Research Service, Publication No. RS22896, dated May 19, 2009.

doctrine. Under the rule of lenity, ambiguities in criminal statutes are construed in favor of the defendant. Application of the merger doctrine avoids the prospect that a defendant would receive two punishments under different statutes for what is essentially a single offense. On February 5, 2009, Senator Leahy introduced S. 386, the Fraud Enforcement and Recovery Act of 2009, which was reported favorably by the Senate Committee on the Judiciary on March 23, 2009, S.Rept. 111-10. On April 28, the bill, as amended, was passed by the Senate. On May 7, an amended version of the bill was passed by the House. It was returned to the Senate, amended, and passed; thereafter, on May 18, it was passed by the House for presentation to the President. The bill includes provisions amending the definition of "proceeds" under the anti-money laundering criminal statutes, 18 U.S.C. § 1956(c)(8) and 1957(c), to specify that the term includes the "gross receipts" of the underlying criminal activity. As passed by the House, the bill also includes a provision addressing the possibility of a merger problem in money laundering prosecutions for predicate offenses closely connected with the elements of the money laundering offense. Other legislation with provisions to cover "gross receipts" includes S. 378 and H.R. 1793.

BACKGROUND OF THE CASE

United States v. Santos[1] involved a challenge to the conviction of the operator of an illegal lottery and one of his collectors for violating a provision of 18 U.S.C. § 1956, a key federal criminal anti-money laundering statute.[2] The defendants were charged with using the "proceeds" of unlawful activity to conduct a financial transaction with intent to promote the illegal gambling business.[3] For a conviction under this particular subsection of the statute, which covers a form of money laundering, referred to as "promotional money laundering," the prosecution must prove: (1) that the defendant engaged in a financial transaction involving the "proceeds" of an unlawful activity; (2) that the unlawful activity had been designated by the statute as a "specified unlawful activity"; (3) that defendant knew that the property involved in the transaction "represents the proceeds of some form of unlawful activity"; and (4) the defendant had the "intent to promote the carrying on of specified unlawful activity."[4]

At their trial, the defendants were convicted of operating an illegal gambling business in violation of 18 U.S.C. § 1955. Under 18 U.S.C. § 1955, anyone convicted of conducting or owning an illegal gambling business is subject to a criminal fine and imprisonment for up to five years. Proof of "illegal gambling business" requires a showing that the gambling business violates state law; involves five or more persons; and has been in operation for more than thirty days or has a gross revenue of $2,000 a day[5] The evidence showed that gambling receipts were used to pay the expenses of the operation–payouts to winners, salaries to employees, costs of betting slips, etc–as well as to realize profits. The promotional money laundering charge was based on payments to winners and to employees–runners–of the gambling business. These payments were part of the underlying charge of operating an illegal gambling business.[6] The defendant convicted of operating the gambling business received a 60-month sentence for the illegal gambling conviction and 210 months for the money laundering.

SUPREME COURT DECISION

The issue presented to the Court was a straightforward question of statutory interpretation: as used in 18 U.S.C. § 1956, does "proceeds" mean "profits" or "gross receipts?" For Santos and his co-conspirators, the answer the Court provided is "profits." For others, however, the answer is not clear because there is no majority opinion in the case; there is an opinion for a plurality of four justices which is joined by a concurring opinion by a fifth justice, Justice Stevens, that limits the reach of the holding to a narrower ground. This means that the case may be cited as authority only for the narrow ground. Complicating this, however, are two factors: (1) the plurality opinion includes language seeking to confine the meaning of Justice Stevens' opinion; and (2) all of the other justices disavowed the approach taken by Justice Stevens.

Justice Scalia, in the plurality opinion, writing for himself and Justices Souter, Ginsburg, and Thomas, found no way to decipher what Congress intended in using the word "proceeds" in 18 U.S.C. § 1956. He found that (1) there is no definition of "proceeds" in 18 U.S.C. § 1956; (2) the federal criminal code does not provide a consistent definition or use for the term; (3) either "profits" or "gross receipts" would fit everywhere "proceeds' is used in the statute; and (3) dictionaries revealed no overwhelming preference for a primary ordinary meaning of the term. Declaring himself unable to resolve the ambiguity, Justice Scalia resorted to the rule of lenity[7] which requires clarity in criminal statutes[8] and ambiguities resolved in favor of defendants.[9] He reasoned that, because "profits" is harder to prove[10] than "gross receipts," defining "proceeds" as "profits" is more lenient towards defendants, and, therefore, it is the required interpretation in the statute. This means that, under this statute, prosecutors must prove, in addition to the other elements of the offense, that the defendant knew that the property involved in the transaction is "*profits*" of "some form of unlawful activity" and that the transaction involves "*profits*" of "specified unlawful activity."[11]

In the opinion, Justice Scalia seeks to dispel arguments raised by the Solicitor General that defining "proceeds" as "profits" undermines the purpose of the money laundering statute– punishing concealment and promotion of illegal activities–because it does not capture all the funds generated by the illegal activity. He first asserts that the purpose of the money laundering laws might well have been eliminating the harm caused by pouring criminal profits into expanded criminal activity, i.e., "leveraging" profits.[12] He, then, notes that the "profits" interpretation avoids the merger[13] problem that would occur in many of the predicate offenses named in 18 U.S.C. 1956, including operating an illegal gambling business in violation of 18 U.S.C. § 1955. This is because, if "proceeds" were interpreted to mean "gross receipts," every separate expense of the underlying crime paid after its commission would be subject to prosecution both as the substantive crime and as the money laundering offense. This would raise the double-jeopardy-like situation[14] that the merger doctrine seeks to prevent.[15]

In a concurring opinion, Justice Stevens essentially limits the reach of the plurality opinion. He did not focus on the rule of lenity although his rationale is consistent with it to the extent that he would interpret "proceeds" to mean "profits" in the case before the Court. He begins with a premise which no other justice embraces–that courts may choose different interpretations of ambiguous terms in statutes depending on the factual circumstances.[16] He draws a parallel between the scope of judicial interpretation of statutes and the power of Congress to flesh out terms in statutes. He concludes that because Congress could specify separate meanings for a term in a statute, courts having to fill in statutory gaps occasioned by ambiguous language do not have to decide on one meaning for all circumstances. To him, the logic is: if Congress may apply different definitions drafting legislation, courts may also do so.[17] From this premise, he seems to have concluded that Congress intended different meanings for "proceeds" in § 1956. Following this conclusion, Justice Stevens finds that "proceeds" is intended to mean "profits" where, as with the predicate offense of conducting an illegal gambling business, there is no legislative history of congressional intent to the contrary.[18] On the other hand, the opinion seems to assert that legislative history of congressional intent is necessary before courts may extend the meaning of "proceeds" to gross receipts. The opinion also contains language indicating that there is the possibility that there is legislative history to substantiate congressional intent to authorize money laundering prosecutions based on gross receipts transactions for certain offenses.[19]

POTENTIAL IMPACT

Although Justice Stevens alludes to the possibility that legislative history supports interpreting "proceeds" as "gross receipts" for some types of prosecutions, it is significant that the plurality opinion disputes this and characterizes it as dicta.[20] This may raise uncertainty as to the sustainability of convictions involving the contraband and organized crime offenses of the kind Justice Stevens cited as having legislative history supporting a "gross receipts" definition of "proceeds." Because many of the money laundering cases that have been brought under the subsection of 18 U.S.C. § 1956 at issue have involved payment of expenses of the underlying crime,[21] the Justice Department's ability to shut off the funding of criminal activities may be severely inhibited. An added problem will be the difficulty of sustaining the burden of proof that will be required to show "profits" of criminal activities. In its merits brief, the Solicitor General argued that this burden would be substantial and perhaps unsurmountable.[22]

In a dissenting opinion, written by Justice Alito, joined by Chief Justice Roberts, and Justices Kennedy and Breyer, there is a further indication of the difficulties that the "profits' definition will present to prosecutors: (1) one of the main purposes of enacting the money laundering laws was to target professional money launderers who are unlikely to know or care whether the property they are dealing with is "profits" or "gross receipts"; (2) a "profits" interpretation would require courts to determine the ordinary expenditures of criminal activities to distinguish them from "profits"; and (3) under the plurality opinion, if the government charges a continuing offense over period of years–as in the case before the Court–the government would have to show that the operation yielded a profit over the course of time charged.

Another dissenting opinion, written by Justice Breyer, who also joined Justice Alito's dissent, alludes to possible solutions to what he, agreeing with the Justices Scalia and Stevens, sees as a merger problem–that prosecutors are able to transform one crime into two and add the money laundering punishments for "financial transactions that constitute an essential part of" the predicate offense.[23] One approach he mentions is requiring that the money laundering transaction be "distinct" from the underlying offense.[24] He also suggests that the merger problem could be corrected by relying on the US Sentencing Commission to use its authority to address the unfairness resulting from using the money laundering statute to under 28 U.S.C. § 991(b)(1)(B).[25] Justice Scalia takes issue with each of these suggestions: the first because "it has no basis whatever in the words of the statute"[26]; the second because it lacks certainty.[27]

LEGISLATION

S. 386, the Fraud Enforcement and Recovery Act of 2009, has been passed by both the House and Senate and, as of May 19, 2009, awaits the signature of the President. It was introduced on February 5, 2009, by Senator Leahy to enhance federal enforcement capabilities to counteract mortgage fraud, securities fraud, and fraud with respect to federal financial assistance. In addition to provisions which provide funding for investigation and prosecution of this type of fraud; substantive provisions extending the reach of specific criminal statutes addressing financial fraud; and (in the version passed by the House) the creation of a legislative branch Financial Crisis Inquiry Commission, the bill includes an amendment to the definition of "proceeds" in the anti-money laundering laws to cover "gross receipts" of the underlying criminal activity. This is designed to solve the problems identified in the *Santos* decision by clarifying the ambiguity found by the Court and making it clear that "proceeds" means "gross receipts." Specifically, as passed by both House and Senate, S. 386 would add the following provision to 18 U.S.C. § 1956(c) and incorporate it into 18 U.S.C.§ 1957(c): "the term 'proceeds' means any property derived from or obtained or retained, directly or indirectly, through some form of unlawful activity, including the gross receipts of such activity." The House-passed version also includes a provision addressing the merger problem. It sets forth a sense of Congress that prosecutions under the major anti-money laundering statutes, 18 U.S.C. §§ 1956 and 1957, should not be undertaken in combination with the prosecution of any other offense, without prior approval of specified Department of Justice Officials or the relevant United States Attorney if the underlying predicate offense for the money laundering prosecution "is so closely connected with the conduct to be charged as the other offense that there is no clear delineation between the two offenses." This provision also includes a requirement that, for the next five years, the Department of Justice provide the House and Senate Judiciary

Committees with annual reports on the prosecutions under such approvals, denied such approvals, and undertaken without such approvals where such approvals would have been relevant.

Other measures in the 111th Congress include: S. 378, introduced by Senator Bayh, as a standalone measure to amend 18 U.S.C. § 1956(c)(8) to specify that "proceeds" includes "gross receipts," and H.R. 1793, introduced by Representative Lungren, to amend 18 U.S.C. § 1956(c) to define "proceeds" as "any property derived from or obtained, directly or indirectly, through the commission of any specified unlawful activity, including the gross proceeds of that specified unlawful activity."

End Notes

[1] (No. 06-1005), 553 U. S ___, 76 U.S.L.W. 4341 (2008), *affirming* 461 F. 3d 886 (7th Cir. 2006). Hereinafter, *Santos*.

[2] See CRS Report RL33315, *Money Laundering: An Overview of 18 U.S.C. 1956 and Related Federal Criminal Law*, by Charles Doyle and Todd Garvey, and CRS Report RS22401, *Money Laundering: An Abridged Overview of 18 U.S.C. 1956 and Related Federal Criminal Law*, by Charles Doyle.

[3] This was the "specified unlawful activity" which formed the predicate for the money laundering charge. "Specified unlawful activity" is defined in 18 U.S.C. § 1956(c)(7)(A) to include racketeering crimes enumerated in 18 U.S.C. § 1961(1), which includes running an illegal gambling business in violation of 18 U.S.C. § 1955.

[4] 18 U.S.C. § 1956(a)(1)(emphasis added). The statute, in pertinent part, provides: (a)(1)Whoever, knowing that the property involved in a financial transaction represents the proceeds of some form of unlawful activity, conducts or attempts to conduct such a financial transaction which in fact involves the proceeds of specified unlawful activity–(A)(i) with the intent to promote the carrying on of specified unlawful activity; or ... (B) knowing that the transaction is designed in whole or in part–(I) to conceal or disguise the nature, the location, the source, the ownership, or the control of the proceeds of specified unlawful activity....

[5] 18 U.S.C. § 1955(b)(1).

[6] Establishing gross revenue of $2,000 is a necessary element of an offense under 18 U.S.C. § 1955. United States v. Reitano, 862 F. 2d 982 (2nd Cir. 1988). Monetary volume constitutes evidence of gross wagering activity, and evidence that a defendant shared in the profits of an illegal gambling business may be used as evidence of conducting the business. United States v. Balistrieri, 577 F. Supp. 1532 (E. D. Wis. 1984).

[7] To invoke the rule of lenity, a court must find that the statute is grievously ambiguous. See Muscarello v. United States, 524 U.S. 125, 138-139 (1998); Staples v. United States, 511 U.S. 600, 619, n. 17 (1994); Chapman v. United States, 500 U.S. 453, 463 (1926).

[8] "[B]efore a man can be punished as a criminal ... his case must be plainly and unmistakably within the provisions of some statute." United States v. Gradwell, 243 U.S. 476, 485 (1917).

[9] "[W]here text, structure, and [legislative] history fail to establish that the Government's position is unambiguously correct ... we apply the rule of lenity and resolve the ambiguity in [the

defendant's] favor." United States v. Granderson, 511, U.S. 39, 54 (1994). *See also* Hughey v. United States, 495 U.S. 411 (1990); United States v. Granderson, 511 U.S. 39 (1994).

[10] In dissent, Justice Alito illustrated some of the problems inherent in requiring prosecutors to prove beyond a reasonable doubt that illegal enterprises have produced "profits" and that those conducting financial transactions for them know that the funds they are using represent the "profits" from some unlawful activity.

[11] 18 U.S.C. § 1956(a)(1).

[12] "A rational Congress could surely have decided that the risk of leveraging one criminal activity into the next poses a greater threat to society than the mere payment of crime-related expenses and justifies the money-laundering statute's harsh penalties." *Santos*, Scalia, J., plurality op. (slip op. 7-8).

[13] For a merger, "[t]he applicable rule is that where the same act or transaction constitutes a violation of two distinct statutory provisions, the test to be applied to determine whether there are two offenses or only one, is whether each provision requires proof of a fact which the other does not." Blockberger v. United States, 284 U.S. 299, 303 (1932).

[14] Justice Stevens raises this issue: "Allowing the Government to treat the mere payment of the expense of operating an illegal gambling business as a separate offense is in practical effect tantamount to double jeopardy, which is particularly unfair in this case because the penalties for money laundering are substantially more severe than those for the underlying offense...." *Santos*, Stevens, J., concurring op. (slip op. 4).

[15] Justice Scalia disputes the effectiveness of the solution to the merger problem suggested by Justice Alito in dissent– limiting "promote" in the statute to exclude expenses of running the criminal activity–both by noting that many of the predicate offenses are not ongoing violations and distinguishing between the kind of evidence that might satisfy the statutory requirement of "intent to promote," from the activity of promoting.

[16] Justice Scalia characterized this approach as unique to Justice Stevens and contrary to precedent, saying that Justice Stevens "relies on the proposition that one undefined word, repeated in different statutory provisions, can have different meanings in each provision .... [which] is worlds apart from giving the same word, *in the same statutory provision, different meanings in different factual contexts.*" *Santos*, Scalia, J., plurality op. (slip op. 15) (emphasis in the original).

[17] Justice Scalia finds this approach inconsistent with Clark v. Martinez, 543 U.S. 371 (2005) (term in immigration law interpreted to apply in one manner to one class of aliens which it covers may not be interpreted in a different manner for other classes of aliens covered). *Id.*

[18] Justice Stevens reinforces the conclusion with respect to requiring "profits" for any money laundering prosecution predicated on operating an illegal gambling business operation. He opines that the result of a prosecution for money laundering (a 20-year felony) based on the kind of business expenses involved in paying winners and employees in connection with an illegal gambling business (a five-year felony) would be "so perverse" that he could not conceive of Congress intending such a result. *Santos*, Stevens, J., concurring, (slip op. 3).

[19] "As JUSTICE ALITO rightly argues, the legislative history of § 1956 makes it clear that Congress intended the term 'proceeds' to include gross revenues from the sale of contraband and the operation of organized crime syndicates involving such sales." *Santos*, (Stevens, J., concurring, slip op. 2-3.). He further adds, "[t]hus, I cannot agree with the plurality that the rule of lenity must apply to the definition of 'proceeds' for these types of unlawful activities." *Id.* 3, n. 3.

[20] *Santos*, Scalia, J., concurring opinion (slip op. 16), notes that no other justice adheres to Justice Stevens' view that one word in one statute may be interpreted different ways in different

case: "... the narrowness of his ground consists of finding that 'proceeds' means 'profits' when there is no legislative history to the contrary.. That is all that our judgment holds. It does not hold that the outcome is different when contrary legislative history does exist."

[21] Brief for the United States, United States v. Santos (No. 06-1005) 3, n. 3 (citing 16 appellate court cases in which money laundering prosecutions were predicated on expense payments rather than profits).

[22] *Id.* 28. Among the factors cited by the government are: poor record keeping on the part of criminals; incentive to falsify records to show losses if money laundering prosecution hinges on profitability of the criminal activity; and, problems that courts will face confronting in devising rules for determining profits and expenses in illegal activities as contrasted with the precise accounting rules for legitimate businesses.

[23] *Santos*, Breyer, J., concurring op. (slip. op. 1).

[24] As authority for this approach Justice Breyer cites United Sates v. Edgmon, 952 F. 2d 1206 (10th Cir. 1991), *cert. denied*, 505 U.S. 1223 (1992). That case was predicated on conversion of property secured by a Farmers' Home Administration loan in violation of 18 U.S.C. § 658. The money laundering charge was based on the concealment prong of the statute, which requires proof that the defendant knew that the financial transaction was designed to conceal "the nature, the location, the source, the ownership, or the control of the proceeds of the specified unlawful activity." 18 U.S.C. § 1956(a)(1)(B)(i). The facts showed that the defendant conspired with his son and sold, as if it were his own, the collateral on which his son had obtained a secured loan. He, then, used the proceeds of the conversion to buy other property on which he obtained a loan and turned those proceeds over to his son. Justice Breyer also appears to suggest that if there was a time difference between the offense and the money laundering that would show that the two are distinct. *Santos*, Breyer, J., concurring op. (slip. op. 1-2).

[25] This section sets forth the purposes of the U.S. Sentencing Commission, one of which is to "provide certainty and fairness in meeting the purposes of sentencing, avoiding unwarranted sentencing disparities among defendants with similar records who have been found guilty of similar criminal conduct...." 28 U.S.C. § 991(b)(1)(B). Another section, 28 U.S.C. § 994(f) requires the Commission, in promulgating guidelines to cover the purposes set forth in 28 U.S.C. § 994(b)(1) particularly.

[26] *Santos*, Scalia J., concurring op. 11.

[27] Id.

INDEX

A

B

C

D

E

F

G

H

I

J

K

L

M

N

O

P

R

S

T

U

V

W